Library of Congress Cataloging-in-Publication Data

Hanc, John.
 The coolest race on earth : mud, madmen, glaciers, and grannies at the
Antarctica marathon / John Hanc. — 1st ed.
      p. cm.
 Includes index.
 ISBN 978-1-55652-738-8
 1. Marathon running—Antarctica. 2. Hanc, John. 3. Runners (Sports)—
Antarctica—Biography. I. Title.
 GV1065.23.A68H36 2009
 796.42'5209989—dc22   2008029677

Interior design: Jonathan Hahn
Title page photo: Brand X Pictures/Steve Allen

Published by Chicago Review Press, Incorporated
814 North Franklin Street
Chicago, Illinois 60610
ISBN 978-1-55652-738-8
Printed in the United States of America
5 4 3 2 1

THE
COOLEST
RACE ON EARTH

Mud, Madmen, Glaciers, and Grannies at the
ANTARCTICA MARATHON

John Hanc

CHICAGO
REVIEW
PRESS

Contents

"It's the last great journey left to man."

—*Ernest Shackleton, prior to leaving on his fateful expedition for Antarctica, 1914*

"Glittering white, shining blue, raven black, in the light of the sun the land looks like a fairy tale, pinnacle after pinnacle, peak after peak—crevassed, wild as any land on our globe, it lies, unseen and untrodden."

—*Roald Amundsen, first man to the South Pole, 1911*

"How do you top this? Maybe a marathon on the moon?"

—*Bobby Aswell, finisher, Antarctica Marathon, 1997*

"Was it a real race? You bet. Toughest damn marathon in the world."

—*Bob Wischnia, finisher, Antarctica Marathon, 1995*

"It takes what I call 'the three Ds' to do a marathon in a place like this: Desire . . . you've got to want to do it. Discipline . . . you've got to train to do it. Dementia . . . you've got to be crazy to do it."

—*Jay Foonberg, finisher, 2003 and 2005 Antarctica Marathon*

AUTHOR'S NOTE

This book is partly a memoir and partly a history of events both recent and distant. What I saw, heard, and did in Antarctica is reported as faithfully as I can. However, a few names have been changed to protect privacy, a few events compressed in time to prevent you from getting bored, and a few moments—come to think of it, maybe even a few miles—of the Antarctica Marathon itself left a bit vague or unaccounted for because I was delirious with pain. Sorry 'bout that.

INTRODUCTION

The wind howled, and a sheet of icy snow pelted the hood of my parka, stinging my eyes. This ferocious storm seemed to have blown in out of nowhere and was now threatening to take me along with it. I knew I had to get out of this as soon as I could.

Oh, how I wished I was back in Antarctica.

Instead, I was trudging through the parking lot of the New York Institute of Technology in suburban Old Westbury. It was March 8, 2005, my first day back to work at the college where I teach journalism and writing, barely forty-eight hours since I had stepped off the plane home after two weeks in Antarctica—and now here I was in the midst of a furious late-winter storm that seemed like something out of the chronicles of a polar explorer, except it was battering Long Island, not the Last Continent.

Down there we had enjoyed calm seas on the irascible Drake Passage and mild temperatures in the bays and inlets of the Antarctic Peninsula. Yet it wasn't the opportunity to sunbathe on the Bellingshausen Sea or swim with seals that had prompted 228 people from fifteen countries to spend an average of five thousand dollars per person and devote two weeks of our lives sailing those remote shores in two converted Russian spy ships. No, we were in Antarctica to run a marathon, a 26.2-mile footrace, held on King George Island, one of the South Shetlands, a chain of islands just off the twelve-hundred-mile-long peninsula that rises out of the Antarctic mainland. In doing so we were representative of a new travel trend that some would say is even crazier than the weather. It involves running really far in really faraway places, places where they don't have six flavors of Gatorade, Nike outlet stores, or even paved roads. From Guam to the Great Wall of China, from Maui to Mount Everest, marathon runners have descended, determined to leave their footprints in corners of the globe that few would have ventured to otherwise.

Think about it: What motivates someone to travel seven thousand miles, spend an almost equivalent number of dollars, and risk a fair amount of unpleasantness (puking from seasickness, bonking from exertion, experiencing hypothermia from awful weather) for the opportunity to run a really long way in a place so inhospitable to life that it barely sustains penguins, seals, and a few species of fungi, much less a stampede of humans clad in Nikes and Gore-Tex? It's not like we had to, after all. If one's intent is to suffer, there are ample opportunities to do so at home, on the job, or in the office of one's dentist or tax adviser. If running 26.2 miles is the goal, New York, Boston, Chicago, and London—heck, almost any major city in the world—offer annual opportunities to do so, in settings far more conducive to the task. On the other hand, if one wants to see exotic sights in extreme places, well, isn't that why they invented the Travel Channel? Trust me—while it was breathtaking, one doesn't really need to go to Antarctica to see what it looks like, especially the part we visited, which in relative geographic terms was what the Caribbean is to the North American mainland, and there the comparison definitely ends.

Why anyone would want to run a marathon in what is frequently called the Last Place on Earth is often the first question asked about this race. For many it seems to start with a deep curiosity about this vast continent, a place that is routinely described as the highest, driest, coldest, and windiest in the world. Almost one and a half times the size of the United States, Antarctica is the fifth largest continent (at 5.1 million square miles, it's bigger than either Europe or Australia) but dead last in terms of population. Look at the list: There's Asia at the top with almost 4 *billion* people. North America is fourth with 501 million. Even Australia/Oceania, next to last, still sounds ready to bust with a population of 32 million. And bringing up the rear—and I mean, really, it's no contest—is Antarctica, whose official population according to WorldAtlas.com is:

Zero.

Yes, an entire continent populated by no one. Of course, that's indigenous population—no one is "from" Antarctica. During its four-month summer, however, there are about four thousand workers on the international scientific bases that dot the continent. These people shuttle in and out, because they would probably go mad (and, as we'll see, many have) trying to live full time in Antarctica. In addition, about thirty thousand tourists now visit over the course of the summer season. That may sound like a large number, but consider that thirty thousand visitors is a modest *day* at Disney World's Magic Kingdom. It's also about nine thousand less than run the New York City Marathon, which is held on one morning in November. And just think, when those thirty-nine thousand people are done running, one block of New York still has a higher population than the entire continent of Antarctica.

Later, some of my compatriots would tell me it was this emptiness—this idea of a great void at the bottom of the Earth—that first captured their imagination, sparking a lifelong interest in Antarctica. For them, it started in grade school, with the idle twirling of the globe that was once a feature of every classroom. Children would notice the blank spot on the bottom. They'd have to tilt the globe or bend down to look up at it. No cities were marked there, no national boundaries, no rivers or lakes. Yet the area was vast, and as opposed to the bright colors of the rest of the globe, it was pure white, as if someone had squirted a blob of Elmer's glue on the bottom of the world and left it there to dry. What kind of place could this be? From that point on, they were determined to find out, to learn the mystery of the void.

I like the idea of these kids, finger on the globe, eyes gazing out the class window, daydreaming about this far-off land of white nothingness. I wish I could say my fascination with Antarctica began in grade school. For me, however, the catalyst came later, much later. Put it this way:

Some men have affairs when they turn fifty. Others go to Vegas. I went to Antarctica to run a marathon.

Yes, it took me almost half a century to decide that I really wanted to do this. Looking back, the urge for some kind of adventure in a really faraway place started as a child growing up in suburban Long Island, New York. I remember reading books about travel to the *North* Pole, but I was only vaguely aware that there was another pole at the bottom of the Earth. The real frontier that intrigued me involved not the blank spaces that cover the top

and bottom of the Earth but the infinitely vast spaces that sur-
round the entire planet.

In May 1961 my first-grade class had gathered in the cafete-
ria with the rest of the children in the aptly named Corona Avenue
Elementary School to watch Alan Shepard go soaring into the
morning sky aboard *Freedom* 7. I sat, mouth agape, no doubt
dribbling milk on my chin. From that moment I had yearned to
be an astronaut. I read everything I could, collected everything
about the space program I could find, and memorized the flight
crew assignments for the Mercury, Gemini, and early Apollo missions. I still know the Gemini teams by heart and will happily
recite them to anyone willing to listen (there are, alas, few takers). No matter, Grissom and Young, Borman and Lovell, McDi-
vitt and White . . . to me, they're as memorable as Orville and
Wilbur or, for that matter, baseball's Tinker, Evers, and Chance
were to earlier generations. I also liked reading the NASA predictions of the time, which ended up in *Life* magazine, or maybe
Highlights for Children—and must have been written by some guy
in the space agency's PR department who was told to just crank
out whatever he dreamed up, because in these articles there was
talk about a lunar base being established by the 1980s, a Mars
expedition in the 1990s, and perhaps the first human colonists on
Mars early in the twenty-first century. I took it all as gospel and
began making plans for my life as a Martian colonist. Being born
in the mid-twentieth century, I thought, was perfect timing! I was
all set for a rewarding career in interplanetary exploration when
I learned that in order to get into astronaut school, you needed
to be really, really good at math. I was really, really bad really,
really early on. And as the math got harder, my dreams of spaceflight went into their own orbital decay.

My disenchantment grew as I got older and the electrifying first Apollo missions turned into the ho-hum later ones where the guys (including my old hero Alan Shepard) played that most conventional of games, golf. Then came Skylab and the Space Shuttle, and while it still gives my heart a rise to watch a launch, American space exploration suddenly became unimaginative, humdrum, and about as appealing as working in a cramped warehouse. It also became increasingly apparent that there would be few if any opportunities for someone like me to ever experience spaceflight, something that had seemed inevitable to me as a kid.

With outer space off the list, my idea of an adventurous place to go became California—where, some would say, many people from outer space actually lived. Alas, plans to drive or hitch there like Jack Kerouac evaporated with my need to obtain gainful employment upon graduation from college (a college, I should add, that did not require math for graduation).

Settling into newspaper work, first at a weekly "alternative" paper in Boston, where I'd gone to college, and later, back home at the big Long Island daily *Newsday*, I was still restless. I'd been running for a few years, mostly to complement my weight training, and I'd begun to enjoy it and demonstrate some very, very modest proficiency in it—meaning, I suppose, that I didn't detest it or pass out while doing it.

In summer 1985 I separated from my wife, and, looking for something to fill the time that had previously been taken up by arguing, I decided to train for a marathon. Just before Labor Day I began my training for the Marine Corps Marathon, held in Washington, D.C., in October. It was an absurdly short time to prepare for a marathon, and the regimen of long runs, track work, and lunchtime runs—we used to change and shower in the pressmen's locker room of *Newsday*, surrounded by two-story-high rolls of newsprint—took their toll. At night, exhausted by the training, alone in my basement apartment, I couldn't do much of anything except sprawl out in front of the TV. What I watched, on my local public television channel, was a seven-part British miniseries based on a famous book by Roland Huntford, *The Last Place on Earth*. This was the riveting (and, I would later learn, highly revisionist) account of the race for the South Pole in 1912 between Roald Amundsen of Norway and English explorer Captain Robert Falcon Scott, the latter of whom died in the attempt. Well-written and well-acted, it was filled with gripping scenes in the Antarctic, which, I began to grasp, was an entire continent. My first marathon turned out to be a Scott-like disaster, with the notable exception that I didn't freeze to death in D.C. I did, however, do almost everything wrong: didn't train long enough (only eight weeks), didn't have a race plan (just went flying out from the start when the gun was fired), never ate breakfast the morning of the race (and bonked). I finished, in great pain, in a time of three hours and fifty-six minutes. As I limped past the Iwo Jima Memorial—the finish line of the race—I swore I'd never run another marathon.

That vow was quickly broken. As it does for many, the marathon had gotten under my skin, and I was determined to get it right. "Everyman's Everest" is how former Boston Marathon winner and *Runner's World* editor Amby Burfoot describes it, the challenge of running considerably farther than is either comfortable or warranted—in the fastest time you can. Fred Lebow, the visionary founder of the New York City Marathon, understood the appeal of the event better than almost anyone. "The marathon is a charismatic event," he said. "It has everything. It has drama. It has competition. It has camaraderie. It has heroism."

And it had me. I was soon a devoted fitness Nazi, training with a group of very talented local runners (all of them more talented than I) who became my close friends and colleagues in our annual marathon quest. The years, and the races, went by. The sting of divorce disappeared; a new and happier union was formed. A child arrived. Middle age was reached, and a career—granted, an unconventional one that involved a sort of mishmash of teaching, writing, and this newfound passion of running—was established. Strangely, the kind of stories I became known for (in a word, *quirky*) allowed me to pursue some of the adventurous travel I had craved as a younger man. Writing for *Newsday*, *Runner's World* magazine, and other publications, I earned a reputation for being willing to train three months and then hop on a plane—or two or three—in order to run 26.2 miles in some very unusual places and then hop back on a plane and write about it. My travels have taken me to a former war zone (Belfast), a formerly Communist capital (Prague), a Civil War battlefield that is supposedly haunted (Chickamauga, Georgia), and a marathon held in the desert outside Roswell, New Mexico, where the heat was so intense that I saw flying saucers orbiting my head at the finish line.

I ran all these marathons, and, oh, just to see what it was like, I was even willing to deliberately *walk* a marathon, one very long day in Phoenix.

In participating in such events, most of them on the margins and outside the throngs that choke the streets of the big-city marathons every weekend of the spring and fall, I began to realize that I was witness to a trend. People were looking for an adventure, and completing a marathon race in an offbeat location seemed to fit the bill, offering the opportunity to view a distant horizon while they went the distance, so to speak.

Of course, you don't need a travel agent to run or walk 26.2 miles. Currently, according to the Web site www.marathonguide .com, there are 384 marathons held every year in the United States and more than 500 internationally. Almost every major U.S. city, and many of the largest cities in Europe, now hosts an annual marathon or half marathon (13.1 miles) race. But while the big, urban marathons, such as New York, Boston, London, or Chicago, attract the largest single-day fields, what www.marathonguide.com termed an "amazing" trend has emerged. According to the Web site's analysis, as of early 2008 the thirty largest marathons accounted for just 57 percent of all finishers (compared to 71 percent as recently as 2006). This, they believe, suggests that the appeal of the sport is trickling down to smaller events and, no doubt, to events in unusual places. Other observers of the sport agree. "It's definitely the case that more marathon runners are looking for opportunities to do their thing in more and more far-flung locations," says Hugh Jones, the London-based secretary of the Association of International Marathons. "Running a marathon offers a ready-made opportunity to connect with the local scene, to meet others from a different background on some kind of common ground."

No ground was more remote or, for that matter, muddier or rockier than that of the marathon held in Antarctica. I'd heard about this race after it was first held in 1995, but it wasn't until four years later that I realized it might represent the way for me to finally do what, on some level, I'd wanted to do since I was a ten-year-old kid with my head in the sky.

What put it all into motion was a phone call I received from a runner named Fred Lipsky.

Like me, Lipsky lives in the New York City megasuburb of Long Island. He had just returned home from an excellent adventure, and he wanted to tell me all about it. This is nothing new: runners and weight lifters and aerobic dancers and karate instructors, or their public relations people, are always badgering me, telling me about some hot, new class they're offering or how they lifted a Mack truck over their heads, completed their first 5K walk, lost fifty pounds, or raised a thousand dollars during a charity walk—and shouldn't that be covered in the paper?

In most cases, the answer is "Congratulations, but . . . no."

Lipsky, however, had done something truly special. He'd been to Antarctica, where he had run . . . a *marathon*. I had heard about this, how some crazy travel agent in Boston had organized a footrace near the bottom of the world. It wasn't until I sat with Lipsky, though, that I began to get jazzed up about it. Diminutive, fast talking, and with a wry sense of humor, he invited me to join him for dinner at a Portuguese restaurant where he was well known and feted like a king, owing to his having patrolled the high-crime neighborhood around the restaurant for years as a beat cop. Over beers and shrimp paella, I listened and scribbled notes as he told me his tale and illustrated it with what appeared to be about a thousand photos he'd taken, many of them showing him standing with penguins. "You wouldn't believe how bad they smelled," he said, his mustache crinkling in disgust.

But penguins were only part of it. Fred told me about swimming in the caldera of an extinct volcano, of partying till dawn as forty-foot waves rocked his ship, of running under the most fantastic of conditions. As I thumbed through the photos, listened to his talking, and sipped my beer, it began to sink in. He'd been there. And he hadn't just gone there—he'd run a marathon there.

"It feels like I just got back from another planet," Lipsky said, shaking his head at the end of his tale of endurance.

I almost dropped my fork. Another planet! A vision of *Freedom* 7 lifting off on that long-ago spring day flashed through my mind—mingling with some blurry recollections of the British miniseries about Scott and Amundsen. Driving home from our dinner that night, the adventure dream, the astronaut dream, reemerged from the margins of my consciousness. This, I thought, would be a way to do it all. At the rate our space program was going, there was no way now that I would ever get an opportunity to orbit the Earth or land on the moon—even as a tourist.

I'd like to say that I ran right out of the restaurant and signed up for the next Antarctica Marathon, but I didn't. Instead I raced home and wrote two thousand words about Lipsky and the smelly penguins, about the race and his experiences. As part of my research, I interviewed Thom Gilligan, the marathon organizer, and read Caroline Alexander's then-new book *The Endurance*, on Ernest Shackleton and his ill-fated but heroic voyage south. The story about Fred Lipsky's excellent adventure appeared on the cover of *Newsday*; the next day it was in the recyclable pile, and I had moved on to the next assignment. But I couldn't stop thinking about the marathon in Antarctica. The race seemed to offer an opportunity to satisfy two great passions in my life, the unfulfilled need for adventure and the urge to run marathons. I realized that this was the opportunity I had been waiting for since I failed the geometry final that drove home the realization that I was too dumb to be an astronaut, ever since I woke up and saw that my life was about to slip away without a proper, new-world, end-of-the-Earth adventure. I had no hope of going into outer space as an astronaut or a billionaire tourist. I was too old and settled to jump into a sports car and drive across the country. I was too chicken to try to climb Mount Everest. But this . . . *this* might fit the bill. A trip to Antarctica, and not "just" a trip, but one in which I would have to do something hard and memorable and, in the process, experience another world.

Here it was—nice, neat, packaged, and laced up like a new pair of running shoes.

I just couldn't pass this up. Still, Phoenix or even Prague was one thing, but to convince my ever-supportive wife that I should be allowed to drop everything and leave her and our young son for two weeks to go to Antarctica, I would need a reason. A good reason. I would need, as we say in the news business, a "peg"— something to hang our story on, some reason why we should be telling this story now, as opposed to next year or two months ago, if at all.

Round numbers and anniversaries are always convenient pegs for such stories, and I suddenly realized I had a good one:

On January 27, 2005, I would turn fifty years old.

One month later, the seventh Antarctica Marathon would be held.

This was my time to do it, to do something crazier than all the crazy marathons I'd done before. But I didn't realize just how many loonies had already landed in Antarctica. Nor did I appreciate what it had taken to make the whole thing possible—a long route traveled by a guy whose own life had, oddly enough, moved on a parallel path with mine for a while. My Antarctica Marathon story can't be told without his.

The Boy Who Walked to the Zoo and Ran to the Ends of the Earth

Tom Gilligan was born to travel—around the block, around the world. "I always wanted to go places," Gilligan recalls. "I'd go any-where."

As a boy, Gilligan ("just like the island," he says whenever asked the spelling of his last name) once walked five miles to the zoo in Stoneham, Massachusetts. Was it simply a way to escape the lower-middle-class neighborhood of Medford, then a drab suburb of Boston best known for being on the route Paul Revere followed on his famous midnight ride? Perhaps. His youthful wanderlust might also have been a response to the crowded conditions of his house—three boys, three girls, and mom, and a square-jawed football-coach father who, in his son's words, "ruled with an iron hand and a leather belt."

In many ways the Gilligan clan was not so different from any of the other mostly Irish and Italian families living in Medford in the postwar years. They didn't come over on the *Mayflower*, and they certainly weren't Brahmins, but they were as embedded in the fabric of the city as the piers sunk into Boston Harbor. Tom's dad, also named Tom, and his mom, Lucille, were high school sweethearts. Tom Sr. was a legendary athlete at Malden Catholic— all-state in both football and baseball. Lucille, who grew up in Medford, attended the girls' Catholic high school nearby. As a 165-pound lineman and placekicker, the elder Tom led Malden Catholic to a championship in the 1930s. Cartoon drawings of him and some of his teammates appeared in the *Boston Globe*—a great honor in those days, when lionizing caricatures of star athletes were a regular feature of the sports pages. Tom Sr. joined the navy when the war broke out, and Lucille followed him, becoming a nurse. He ended up getting wounded in North Africa, and after recuperating was on his way to the Pacific when, during a brief stopover in San Diego, he and Lucille got married. After the war he did what many young men did in that era: he got a job with the phone company, New England Telephone. It was the type of position that would guarantee a steady income, benefits, and a pension. He worked his days as a repairman, and on nights and weekends he returned to the gridiron as the coach of his old team, Malden Catholic, leading his alma mater to another Catholic League Championship.

Tom and Lucille had six kids and raised them in a four-bedroom house with one bathroom. The town they lived in was known by locals as "Meffa"—that's "Medford" the way a tough guy, a mafioso with a "Bahstan" accent, might pronounce it, gulping down the word and swallowing the *d*'s like cups of hot espresso. However it was pronounced, Medford was a tough town, divided into different ethnic enclaves: the Italians in South Medford, the Irish Catholics in the north, the African Americans in the western part of town. But each neighborhood was proud and close knit. "It's not like there were gang fights, but we were competitive with one another," says Dave McGillivray, a friend of Gilligan's who also grew up there. "People took pride in their territories, their sports, and their ethnicity."

Young Tom had another source of pride—and sometimes frustration. Growing up as the son of Tom Gilligan Sr., the football star, the football coach, there were certain expectations. You weren't going to cry when you fell down, and you were going to play a contact sport. For Tom Jr.—who also attended Malden Catholic—that sport was hockey. Everyone knew that Coach Gilligan's son was going to be hard, and he was. Especially on defense, which in any sport is what the blue-collar guys gravitate toward. "I was pretty tenacious," Gilligan recalls. "I worked hard at it."

The year before Gilligan joined, Malden Catholic's hockey team had won the Catholic school championship—a big deal in that part of the country. They took the game seriously, and for Tom Jr. that included staying in shape in the off-season. When his hockey teammates joined the cross-country team, he was encouraged to follow along. He did, reluctantly; running was painful.

"I hated it," he says. "I was doing it for hockey."

While Tom flourished on the ice and dreamed of wandering far afield, his future, like that of most of the families around him, seemed preordained. "I was being bred to go to work for a big company," he said. That was where the union jobs were, the protected jobs, the jobs that a man could rely on to help him when he was ready to settle down, start a family, and move into a house—probably a row house like all the others that seemed to dot the neighborhoods of Boston.

The problem for Tom, and a lot of young men and women in the 1960s, was that he didn't want to do any of that, a point over which he and Tom Sr. clashed. "He was a staunch union guy, and I was very, very independent," he says. "I wanted to be more entrepreneurial, even though I didn't know that word existed back then." Tom went to college—but not some exclusive, leafy private school. He took night classes at Northeastern University, in a working-class section of Boston. After three semesters there, young Tom transferred to Merrimack College in North Andover, where he earned a degree in marketing. He graduated in 1972 and landed an interview with a large insurance company, Provident Mutual Life. The insurance industry ruled in Boston back then; insurance companies were the ones responsible for the city's largest buildings, the Prudential Center and, later, the John Hancock Tower, which for a few years was famous because of a design flaw that occasionally caused its windows to fall out.

Gilligan got a job as a sales trainee. This was the kind of job that young men from large Irish Catholic families in Medford were supposed to get—and be grateful for getting. He quit after eight months. "I learned quickly what I did not want to do for the rest of my life," he says. Tom wanted to walk to the zoo again. He wanted to wander—and while Boston is as much a part of him as his chowder-thick accent, he knew he wanted to go a lot farther than Meffa. When he saw an ad in the *Globe* for what was then called BOAC—now British Air—he immediately responded. The airline was expanding its office in Boston and was looking for sales trainees. They hired twelve people in March 1973, and Gilligan was one of them. For the next three years he learned the travel business. "We trained first as ticket agents, working at the ticket counters at Logan," he said. "I loved it from day one."

During the slow winter travel season, BOAC laid off Gilligan and its other trainees. He didn't mind; he went up to New Hampshire to ski for a couple of months. This schedule continued for the next three years. Seven months with the airline followed by five months on unemployment, November–March. Perfect for ski season. "It was one of the most fun periods of my life," he says. In the besotted 1970s, that meant sex, drugs, and rock and roll. "Oh yeah," he adds, almost as an afterthought, "and skiing." The exception to this snow-peaked bacchanalia came one day when the roads were clear and he didn't feel like heading over to the lodge. Instead he impulsively went for a run, something he had not done since high school. "I went two miles," he said. "It felt OK. So two days later, I ran four miles."

Back home in spring 1976, Gilligan decided to start jogging regularly to combat the effects of five months of winter fun in New Hampshire. He went over to the aptly named Marathon Sports store in Cambridge to buy a pair of shoes—not sneakers but new, so-called running shoes. Tom picked up a pair manufactured in Oregon by a fledgling outfit named Nike. While he was trying them on, he bumped into an old friend from college, Paul Sullivan, a runner who had even started to enter local road races. Sullivan convinced Tom to join him.

Most first-time road racers start with something relatively short, typically a 5K run (5 kilometers, or 3.1 miles). But this was the beginning of the 1970s "running boom," when it seemed as if every upwardly mobile young man in America was lacing up his shoes to follow in the footsteps of Frank Shorter, the Yale-educated lawyer who had won the gold medal in the Olympic marathon in 1972. For these guys, more was better. So when Gilligan agreed to train with his friend for their race, it was not a 5K or even a 10K (6.2 miles); it was a 20K—about 12 miles. "I said, 'Wow! That's a long way. But we'll give it a try.'" They trained together for a few weeks and then showed up at the start of the race, which turned out to be 25K—over 15.5 miles. "I said, 'I can't go this far!'" recalled Gilligan. "My friend said 'just inhale and exhale and you'll get through.'" He did. Halfway through, Gilligan thought to himself, *This is torture. I'm never doing it again.* But the minute he crossed the finish line, he underwent a major attitude adjustment. "I said, 'This is fun. I can't wait to do it again.' I was hooked."

Gilligan became a running bum—a corollary to the ski variety and a well-recognized species in the Boston area in the late 1970s. The city had become the hub for running on the East Coast. It already had the most prestigious race in the world, the Boston Marathon, and one of the finest clubs in the country, the Greater Boston Track Club. The Boston area was also home to several new running shoe manufacturers, Etonic, Saucony, and New Balance, all pumping out pairs of durable-but-light trainers for all the running boomers. And they had the right demographics—lots of bright, "type A," goal-oriented young men (and a few women) who wanted the kind of robust, physical challenge they weren't getting in their classrooms, their downtown law offices, or their positions in the emerging high-tech businesses along Route 128.

Gilligan, who had watched the Boston Marathon with his father many times as a kid, set his sights on going 26.2 miles, which he did with success. Although he crashed and burned in his first Boston Marathon, his compact five-foot nine-inch, 155-pound frame was well suited for running; soon he had joined the elite Greater Boston Track Club, coached by the charismatic Billy Squires, a college track coach and former all-American runner at Notre Dame. Gilligan was now training with the likes of Bill Rodgers, next to Shorter, the greatest American marathoner of his generation; Joan Benoit, who would go on to win the gold in the first Olympic women's marathon in 1984; Greg Meyer, the last American man to win the Boston Marathon (which he did in 1983); Lynn Jennings, later an Olympian; Tom Derderian, an outstanding runner and coach who later wrote the definitive history of the Boston Marathon; Dave McGillivray, another man from "Meffa" who is now race director for the Boston Marathon; and a speedy, young registered nurse from Children's Hospital named Sharon O'Hagan, who would eventually become Mrs. Tom Gilligan.

Under the tutelage of Squires, the members of the Greater Boston Track Club (GBTC) did repeats up Heartbreak Hill so many times that they could have run it in their sleep. They also worked together to improve. "You did whatever it took," wrote Barbara Huebner in a 2004 article on the GBTC's history in *American Track & Field*. "You shared what you had. You kicked around ideas. And you succeeded." They really were a team, and not just on the track: members of the club ate together, drank together, partied together, and eventually lived together. "We had a house in Wellesley," Gilligan said. "Right on the fifteen-mile mark of the marathon course."

The members of the GBTC were the finely honed peak of a competitive and single-minded movement. Although they had cardiovascular systems as finely tuned as NASCAR engines, the running boomers were less interested in fitness than they were in racing and having fun. Nobody lifted weights or took yoga classes; *cross training* wasn't even a marketing slogan yet, much less a recommended approach to exercise. The serious boomers ran almost every day, sometimes twice a day. They ran more miles in a week than most people put on their car odometers, then raced on the weekends and figured that with all that training they could eat—and drink—whatever they wanted. So they did.

The attitude was perfect for the 1970s and, in the case of Gilligan and his running cronies, perfect for Boston—a city that in the mid-to-late 1970s supported two alternative newspapers, a nascent punk rock scene, and tens of thousands of college students (me among them). Most of the students were too busy rolling joints and blasting their stereos out the dorm windows along Commonwealth Avenue to want to run, but on the third Monday in April, thousands would gather along the road to watch and cheer on the runners in the Boston Marathon. Many of the top competitors in those years were members of the GBTC, which by then had achieved a national reputation in the sport. The club earned its place in running mythology when in 1979 it claimed four of the top ten spots at Boston (led by Rodgers, who won the marathon).

Those who were there speak nostalgically of the era when runners ran rampant in Boston. They were a high-profile, exotic subculture, like the hippies of a decade earlier, except without psychedelics. It was a tight, almost communal society. "There was a terrific passion and a certain innocence pervading the sport, and it really flowered more in Boston than anywhere else in America," recalls Rodgers, who became so linked to the Boston Marathon (a race he won four times) and the city's running scene that he earned the nickname "Boston Billy." "We felt that anything was possible," he says. "And we had so much fun following through on that."

Whenever runners today hear that Gilligan actually trained with the likes of Rodgers and Meyer, they conclude that he must have been an Olympic-caliber runner. "I just laugh," he says. "I was lucky to make the D team of the Greater Boston Track Club. I could run 2:30 in the marathon . . . these guys all ran 2:12 or under." Some perspective is needed here: in no other sport is the word *good* more relative than in marathoning. Gilligan's 2:30:42 might have been twenty minutes slower than a world-class performer like Rodgers; however, it would be good enough to win most local marathons today. Any American recreational runner who can complete 26.2 miles in the low three-hour range is considered outstanding today—and *good* now means you can break four hours!

The world of running was going to change dramatically in the next decade. In the early 1980s, Huebner writes, the fast-growing running shoe companies lured many of the Greater Boston Track Club's top runners to their own teams, and the club faded. Many of the original running boomers eventually burned out—casualties of too many miles, too much racing, and too many overuse injuries. They would be followed by a wave of marathon runners whose numbers were far greater but whose times were much slower. Consider that in 1980, 120,000 Americans crossed the finish line of a marathon. About 90 percent of them were men, and their median finish time was 3 hours and 32 minutes. Twenty-five years later, the number of finishers nearly quadrupled, to 432,000 finishers, 41 percent of them female. The median time for men in 2005 had shot up to 4 hours and 20 minutes; the typical female finisher took 4 hours and 51 minutes. This was a different breed than gazelles like Gilligan and his pals on the Greater Boston Track Club, who logged eighty miles a week and ran 2:20 marathons. The second-generation running boomers did not typically have high school or collegiate running backgrounds. Indeed, many of them had no athletic background at all. Unlike the first generation, they tended not to party hearty. As with so many aspects of our society, running in the 1990s was a little more sober and serious than in the 1970s. For this new cadre of runners, the marathon would be a route to fitness, weight loss, self-actualization, fundraising for worthy causes . . . or travel.

That's where, Gilligan says, "I was a classic example of being in the right place at the right time."

The route that got him to that place—and from there to the shores of Antarctica—began in June 1977. At that time Gilligan was working for a travel "wholesaler," a firm that packaged and sold tours to travel agents. He had jumped at the opportunity, a job that would provide a chance for him to combine his college degree in marketing with the travel basics he'd learned at the airline. He diligently spent his time trying to pitch travel packages to the Bahamas to rich doctors and corporations looking for a warm place to hold their annual stockholder meetings.

About ten months into the new job, he got an idea—to somehow combine his business (travel) with his passion (running). Gilligan and McGillivray had decided to run the Honolulu Marathon, held that December. "I said to Dave, 'Let me put together a package and see if we can get some people interested.' I thought it would bring in a little business for the company." Also, that way he and McGillivray could save a little money on their trip. So he typed up a flyer, made some photocopies on yellow paper, and handed them out at the Falmouth Road Race in Cape Cod that August. RUN THE HONOLULU MARATHON IN DECEMBER, the flyer read. AND LET US TAKE CARE OF THE TRAVEL ARRANGEMENTS. The price: $599. He got six takers. That December he, McGillivray, and his first six clients flew to Honolulu with airline tickets purchased by Gilligan, stayed in hotels rooms booked by Gilligan, and ran the marathon in which Gilligan had registered them.

On the morning of the race, they rode a bus to the start. Another passenger heard them talking and asked the runners where they were from. "Boston," Gilligan replied. The passenger looked shocked: "What are you doing here?" Gilligan replied that they had come from Boston to run the Honolulu Marathon. Eyebrows all over the bus raised in surprise. That's how novel this idea was . . . people traveling to a marathon. The next fall Gilligan decided to try again, this time with a race closer to home. He chartered a bus to take interested runners to the 1978 New York City Marathon. He'd also handle their registration and hotel bookings. He printed up another flyer and handed it out at a couple of local races. "We got ninety people, two busloads full, in the wink of an eye," Gilligan recalled. "That's when I realized we were onto something."

The problem was that his employer didn't. After New York, Gilligan was in the midst of making plans for a third trip, this one to a marathon in Montreal, when his boss called him in. "You're spending all your time booking trips for runners," he said. "I want you to go back to getting corporate accounts."

"But I think this running thing has a future in it," Gilligan replied.

"OK," said his boss. "If that's how you feel, clean out your desk. I'll give you three weeks severance." It couldn't have come at a worse time. While they were on the trip to Montreal, Gilligan's father died, at age sixty-two. He was now out of a job and on his own. He had less than a thousand dollars to his name. At the same time, the Barbizon Hotel in Manhattan was demanding a down payment for the twenty-five rooms he had booked to accommodate the runners for his second New York City Marathon trip. "They wanted five hundred dollars," Gilligan recalled. "I said, 'Look, I'm just starting a new company. Could you take my Master Card?'" The hotel wanted a company check. "I said, 'They're being printed.' They weren't. The hotel said, 'Well, what's the name of your company?' I blurted out, 'Marathon Tours.'"

The hotel finally agreed, and Gilligan started his new company using his Master Card and half of the money he had in the world. "I said to myself, *OK, I've got a name for my company. Now I've got to get out there and fill this bus so that we're still in business a month from now.*"

They were. Over the next decade, Marathon Tours would grow from weekend charter buses bound for the New York City Marathon to planes full of runners jetting thousands of miles to the marathons that began to spring up in London, Paris, and Rome . . . all the way to the Great Wall of China. Gilligan, the kid with wanderlust from Medford, eventually became a rich man, with homes in Cape Cod and Maui. He never stopped traveling—he continued to accompany his clients on most of the trips—but he did begin to cater to the members of the second generation of the running boom, the runners who did it not for fast times but for good times: memorable experiences and self-fulfillment. "Tom

was a genius in sensing this," says Bill Rodgers, who accompanied Gilligan and a group of his runners to Marathon Tours' first
European trip, the Stockholm Marathon in 1981. "We had a terrific trip," recalls "Boston Billy," who finished first. "Winning the
race made it even sweeter!"

Something else happened in Sweden. While visiting the town
hall in Stockholm, Gilligan wandered into the room where the
city council meets. And everyone had a name plaque at his or her
seat. Many of those plaques had TOM written on them. He asked
his guide, "Are there a lot of people here named Tom?" She
laughed and explained that *tom* is the Swedish word for "empty."
"I didn't want to have a name that means empty. So I decided to
add an *h*."

What would Tom Gilligan have said about Thom Gilligan?
"My father would have said, Here's just another example of you
being rebellious." (One senses that Coach Gilligan might have
been even blunter in his assessment and language.)

Yet the father had clearly passed on his blue-collar work ethic
to his son, now a rising star in the big city. Even as the business
grew bigger, the logistics more involved, Thom was hands-on.
Again, like most successful coaches, he wasn't always loved, and
his style was about as warm and fuzzy as the streets of Medford
in January. Still, he worked hard to provide the services and the
experience his customers—all runners like himself—deserved.

Essentially, though, Gilligan's job was to deliver those customers to the starting lines of faraway events organized by other
people.

That changed in 1993 when a magazine story extolling Gilligan's success would spark his most ambitious project—and almost
put him out of business.

The Last Race on Earth

By the early 1990s, Marathon Tours and Travel was a three-million-dollar-a-year business, handling seven thousand clients annually. Gilligan was organizing package tours to marathons in Berlin, Paris, Athens, Bermuda, Stockholm, and Venice—as well as Chicago, Boston, and New York. His lucrative but unusual niche attracted the attention of the industry newsweekly *Travel Agent*. In 1993 the magazine deemed Gilligan's business sufficiently newsworthy to plaster his face on the cover of its August issue. "Pace Setter," read the headline. "Tom [*sic*] Gilligan runs circles around the competition by handling the specialty market of competitive runners."

The two-page story traced the history of Marathon Tours, the market for runners, and destination marathons. In it Gilligan explained how he was different from other travel agents. "I don't look at myself as a booking agent for runners," he said. "I look at myself as a runner who shows other runners where to go."

Gilligan's clients were certainly going places, *Travel Agent* reported, quoting Gilligan as saying that he sent clients to "every continent except Antarctica." Thinking back on it years later, Gilligan chuckles at that quip, saying, "I meant nothing by it." But within days of the publication of the article, he got a call. "This guy said, 'Would you like to have a marathon in Antarctica?' I said, 'Who is this nut?'"

His name was Sam Blyth, and he was the owner of the Toronto-based corporation Marine Expeditions. Blyth wanted to expand his business to Antarctica, a place that until the late 1980s or so was about as likely a tourist destination as Mars. But a trickle of tourists—environmentalists, bird- and whale-watchers, adventure seekers—had started to seep into the continent at the bottom of the Earth. Blyth had the ships to get them there; now all he needed was his own group of willing tourists. He sent two of his representatives to Boston to make a pitch to Gilligan. They met in his office and explained to Gilligan how such a trip could be done affordably yet profitably. At that time, it cost at least fifteen thousand dollars to visit the continent, but Marine Expeditions had a better formula: They had purchased some converted Russian research vessels at auction. During the cold war these had been so-called listening ships, designed to keep an ear to American submarine activity. The ships came complete with the crews, who worked for post–cold war Russian wages, which enabled the company to keep costs down and which translated into a far more affordable cost for tourists. Gilligan was intrigued. The economics seemed to make sense. But there was still one basic question: Was it feasible? Marine Expeditions seemed capable of getting a boatload of runners to Antarctica, but then what? Could a marathon be held in Antarctica? And if so, where?

A quick geography refresher: When most Americans think about Antarctica, they think of a howling, frozen ice plain, polar bears, igloos, and maybe, if they've watched too many cartoons, a red-and-white barber pole sticking out of the snow to mark the point of the South Pole. In fact, there are no polar bears (they live only in the Arctic), and the climate in most parts of Antarctica is so hostile that there are no indigenous land mammals at all. And no people, so no igloos, either. (However—hold on to your earmuffs!—the barber pole is actually there, which shows that you have to have a sense of humor to go to Antarctica, despite how unwelcoming it is.)

Gilligan decided to take a look for himself. He booked passage on one of the existing tourist cruises to Antarctica. Like most of the other privileged few who had visited the continent at that point, he found the experience profound and transcendent. "I was totally overwhelmed by the sheer, pristine beauty and by the power of nature in this environment," said Gilligan. "You see that here in its rawest sense." During his trip Gilligan arranged to visit three places that had been suggested to him as possible sites for the marathon. They were all located along or just off the Antarctic Peninsula, the thick tentacle of land that sweeps up from the West Antarctic coast into the Southern Ocean, pointing toward the Shetland Islands and beyond it South America. This was and still is the destination for most of the steadily growing number of tourists. The Shetlands and the peninsula are a little closer, a little less extreme, and thus a lot less expensive than visiting the Antarctic mainland, which is covered in a thick crust of ice almost year-round. There, life has a precarious foothold in Antarctica. Owing to the slightly moderating effects of the sea, this part of the continent does have a summer season—the "austral" summer, which runs from November to February—during which time temperatures hover around freezing. Along the shores and islands of the peninsula region, a few hardy species of plants can be found, along with penguin rookeries, bird habitats, and seal colonies. Each of the proposed sites had one of the basic requirements needed for the marathon: the presence of a nearby research station (of which there are many in internationally "owned" Antarctica), meaning that, in case of an emergency, medical help would not be far off. Also, basic necessities such as running water and toilets would be available.

The first place Gilligan visited was called Arctowski, the Polish base in Antarctica. But when he went for a "test run" near the Arctowski base, along the beach and up into the hills, he wasn't pleased. The footing was too poor, the ground muddy. "Unreliable," he said, crossing it off the list. The second choice was King George Island, then the site of four research stations: Chinese, Russian, Uruguayan, and Chilean. There were some crude roads linking the bases, which could be used as part of a marathon course. Plus, part of the island was covered by the Collins Glacier, an ice sheet that partially melted in the austral summer. "The idea of running on a glacier sounded pretty cool," said Gilligan. He was sold on King George Island until he saw Esperanza, the main Argentine station. Located on the very tip of the Antarctic Peninsula, adjacent to the Hope Sea (*esperanza* is the Spanish word for "hope"), this seemed to be the ideal spot: a beautiful base built at the water's edge amid towering mountains that surrounded a huge glacial plane. "They took me up there in a half-track," said Gilligan. "I got out and ran and ran. The views were spectacular."

Gilligan decided that Esperanza would be the place for the first organized sports event ever held in Antarctica. There was another plus to Esperanza, or so it seemed at the time: Gilligan and Blyth's deputy, Pat Shaw, could deal directly with one country—Argentina—as opposed to King George Island, where they would have to negotiate, in effect, with four different nations. Politically, Antarctica is like Switzerland without bankers. It's neutral in the most basic sense, since there are no indigenous people, no citizens of Antarctica to vote one way or the other. By treaty, the continent is jointly managed by the international community. But, as in every other international venture, nationalistic pride plays a role, as Gilligan soon learned when dealing with the Argentines. "They referred to Esperanza as 'our country,'" he said. "They would say, 'Yes, we'd love to help you stage a marathon in our country.' I kept thinking, *Well, it's not really your country, is it?*" Gilligan would later learn that the Argentines' attitude toward their claim in Antarctica has annoyed other countries, particularly the British, who fought the closest thing to an Antarctic War when they clashed with the Argentines in 1982 over the sub-Antarctic Falkland Islands in the South Atlantic.

Gilligan was a travel agent, not a UN envoy, so he kept his mouth shut. At first the Argentines seemed eager to cooperate. They liked the idea of having one of their bases as the site of the marathon and all the attendant publicity that was likely to generate. They liked the idea of one hundred or so tourists flying to Buenos Aires, and then shuttling—on Argentine airlines—to Ushuaia, the city at the southern tip of Argentina and the launching point for most Antarctic expeditions. They liked the thought of these tourists spending their dollars in Argentina while en route to their crazy marathon. They liked everything. It looked like a go.

Gilligan put an announcement for the new race in the Marathon Tours newsletter. "I called it the Last Marathon," he said, "because I felt it was the last place on Earth anybody would think of running a marathon." He still wasn't sure he would get enough interest to justify the expense of organizing the trip. He was wrong. "The response was unbelievable," he said. "We sold out two ships . . . 159 people . . . in ninety days." The cost was about thirty-five hundred dollars per person, not including airfare.

One of those who responded was Ed Sylvester, then a fifty-eight-year-old civil engineer from Nevada City, California. Sylvester had started running in the early 1980s and had traveled with Marathon Tours to Europe. His wife, Bernadette, often accompanied him. "I was game to do all kinds of interesting things," Sylvester recalls. As soon as he saw the ad, he showed it to Bernadette, who collected penguin "stuff."

"Somebody's trying to do a marathon in Antarctica," he said.

"We're going," replied Bernadette.

On the other side of the North American continent, in Bedford, Nova Scotia, Roger Churchill had a similar reaction. He and his wife, Paula, had met Gilligan in Athens, in October 1993. The Churchills were there so that Roger could run the marathon, but they had planned the trip on their own. The night before the race, the couple was strolling down the street looking for a place to eat dinner and saw a group of North American runners outside their hotel. "I asked them, 'How are you getting to the race start tomorrow?'" Churchill recalls. "They said, 'Our leader, Thom Gilligan, is over here; maybe he has space on the bus.' We went over and introduced ourselves to him." Gilligan invited the Churchills to ride the bus they had chartered to the start, twenty-six miles outside Athens, on the plains of Marathon. Paula could come, too. Oh and by the way, Gilligan added, he and his group were having a post-marathon party the next night and the Churchills were invited to join them. The next night, as they celebrated their marathon, Gilligan mentioned to Churchill his Antarctica plan. The Canadian was fascinated. "I thought, *My God, that's going to be some great adventure.* Paula loves these spots that are new and exciting. She was for it right away; so was I."

Once the ouzo wore off and he was back in Nova Scotia, however, Churchill had his doubts. "I thought, *Well, they're nice guys and everything, but a marathon in Antarctica? Come on.*" By spring 1994, Churchill admits, he'd "certainly" forgotten about it. That's when Gilligan called and told him the trip was on. "I said, 'Count me in,'" Churchill recalls. Roger and Paula were excited. The rest of Nova Scotia was incredulous. "I didn't know anybody from my community who had been to Antarctica," he said. "A lot of people didn't even really know where it was." Once it became apparent that they were going ahead with this, that Roger Churchill, respectable banker from Halifax, and his equally respectable wife, Paula, were going to go—where? to do what? run a marathon? in *Antarctica?*—their family stepped in. "They encouraged us to make sure our wills were up-to-date. I also think certain members of the family had picked out what pieces of furniture they were going to get from our house once we never came back."

While the Churchills' extended family was skeptical, Gilligan was feeling pretty good about this seemingly far-fetched idea. As 1994 came to a close, everything seemed ready. The runners' deposits were in, the ships were booked, and the flight arrangements were made. It was Christmas Eve, and Gilligan was ready to celebrate what might be the crowning success of his career. Who knew what this could lead to? Another cover story in *Travel Agent*, at least. Then he heard the hiss and squawk of his fax machine. It was a letter from Buenos Aires. The foreign minister of Argentina had overruled the tourism and finance officials. Probably envisioning a group of ugly Americans leaving their PowerBar wrappers and empty Gatorade bottles on the beaches of Esperanza, he had denied permission to hold the marathon on "their" soil. Gilligan was dumbfounded. "This was a month before we were going to leave," he said, angrily. "This was a done deal."

Just then the phone rang. It was Pat Shaw, calling on a cell phone. He was on his way to South America and had heard the news. "I said, 'Pat, what are we going to do?'" Gilligan recalled. "He said, 'Well, we're not going to have a marathon in Argentina, but we *are* going to have a marathon in Antarctica.'" While Shaw negotiated, Gilligan fretted. "I spent that Christmas wondering how we were going to refund the money, whether I'd have to go out of business," he said. "It was horrible." But two days later, Shaw called again. He had established contact with King George Island, one of the original sites they had visited. Long discussions ensued, as Shaw visited each of the four major research stations and met with representatives of four different governments. All were ecstatic about the idea of hosting a marathon on the island. It had nothing to do with borders and everything to do with boredom. "Scientific research of the type done at these stations can be incredibly dull," Gilligan said. "You count penguins; you check the weather." Day after day after day. Same routine, same food, same few co-workers. "The idea of a hundred or so people coming down to participate in a race was very exciting," he said.

Finally, in January, Shaw called Gilligan to report that all four countries had granted official permission. "But," he added, "you'll have to finalize everything during the trip." Gilligan, his staff, and the runners arrived in Buenos Aires and then flew to Ushuaia, at the southern tip of Argentina. There they boarded the ships—the

Akademik Ioffe and *Akademik Sergey Vavilov*—for the two-day voyage across the treacherous Drake Passage. Gilligan's stomach was in a knot, and it wasn't because of the waves that pounded his "flagship," the *Ioffe*. (They actually had a calm voyage down—coming back would be a different story, as twenty-five-foot waves rocked their ships.) Gilligan still had no idea exactly what the marathon course would be. He knew it would be on King George Island; he knew that it would probably be held, in part, on the dirt roads connecting the bases, and that they would climb the glacier. But when marathon runners go to a race, they expect an accurately measured and marked 26.2-mile course; they expect start and finish lines and a clock at the finish. All that had yet to be worked out. "People on the ship were asking me, 'What's the course like?'" he said. "And I just BSed my way through it. I said, 'Oh, it's nice. Some streams, some hills, some glacier.'" As it turned out, that was a fairly accurate description, except for the "nice" part. While the scenery was in some parts breathtaking, most of these runners would have little breath left to take: the Last Marathon would turn out to be one of the most grueling and difficult endurance runs ever staged.

On February 5, after the crossing of the Drake and a couple of days exploring sights that would become familiar to the participants in subsequent Antarctica Marathon trips—glaciers, volcanoes, abandoned whaling stations along the peninsula—the ships anchored off King George Island.

The runners in the first edition of this event were mostly male and North American, although there were a number of spouses who came along, partially out of curiosity and partially, one presumes, because if their husbands were crazy enough to do something like this, they wanted to be there, just in case. The runners ranged in age from seventeen to seventy-four and included John Cahill, a seventy-one-year-old millionaire hotelier from Salt Lake City, and Wally Herman, a sixty-nine-year-old Canadian who had run 432 marathons in his career. Gilligan had come over to the island the night before, and based on his exploratory run there of a year or so earlier, had quickly mapped out a course, which turned out to be a mile longer than the regulation 26.2-mile marathon distance.

The mood on the ships the morning of the race was giddy. Runners wondered what to expect, wondered about the course and if the marathon would even come off successfully. Bernadette Sylvester, who had already been happily photographed with penguins, caught the mood perfectly when she showed up in the dining room wearing a sweatshirt that read, MY NEXT HUSBAND WILL BE NORMAL. At about 9 A.M., the runners and the support crew climbed into the Zodiacs—small outboard-driven landing craft of the type made famous by French underwater explorer Jacques Cousteau—and buzzed across the choppy waters to the shore, where they were greeted by the commander of the Uruguayan base. It was there that 104 runners would assemble to run the first Last Marathon.

When the runners got their first glimpse of King George Island, Churchill recalled, there was "a sense of disappointment." Instead of a fantasy world of ice, the runners looked out on a bleak landscape of brown sprinkled with a cluster of buildings that looked as if they'd been airlifted from a down-on-its-luck Rust Belt town. Plus, the weather was over thirty-two degrees Fahrenheit. "I think we all expected to be running in a blinding snowstorm," Churchill recalled. Ice, snow, or no, they were in Antarctica and only a shoelace's width away from a fiasco. "Just the right element of danger hung over the course," said *Runner's World* senior editor Bob Wischnia, who ran that day and later wrote about the experience for the magazine. "It was marked but not well marked, and we all knew that getting lost could prove fatal." Although the temperatures were well above freezing, that wasn't necessarily good news: some of the ice on the glacier had melted in the warm temperatures, turning the primitive roads on the island into what Wischnia described as "ankle-deep, shoe-sucking mud."

Things did go wrong. The wind blew away the little orange flags that had marked the route, leaving runners uncertain as to the course, which involved running up and down the glacier not once but twice. The ATVs that were supposed to help Gilligan and his race crew buzz around the island conked out. And then there was the mud: Churchill remembers being shocked by its severity. "The race starts and suddenly, I'm up to my ankles in mud," he said. "I ran the first couple of miles and felt like I'd gone fifteen or twenty."

"We were slipping and sliding on the ice and occasionally breaking through icy streams up to our knees," runner Pete Baker later told his local paper, the *San Jose Mercury News*. "When I got to the top of the glacier, I thought, *Thank God that's over.* And then came the climb over the boulders, followed by an eight-mile muddy dirt road that literally sucked your shoes off. It was the hardest race I've ever run."

Amid the mud and the rocks, the runners were reminded of what had enticed them there when they passed Admiralty Bay, filled with massive icebergs, pack ice, and seals and penguins cavorting on the beach. "Indescribably beautiful," Wischnia called it. And the goal was to keep it that way. Whatever fears the Argentines may have had about Americans trashing the joint were unfounded. The philosophy of the Last Marathon was similar to those of many other eco-adventurers: leave the land the way you found it. In Antarctica that was more than the spirit—it was international law, and the race organizers intended to abide by it. "You can't spit, you can't pick up a pebble, you can't leave anything or take anything," said one of the runners, Pat Bernson, a personal trainer from New York City. The environment was not only pristine, of course, but also precarious: there were two casualties, one questionable, one potentially fatal.

First, a runner claimed to have slipped and fallen into a shoulder-deep crevasse. Gilligan, who had carefully inspected the glacier before the start and had found no crevasses, was skeptical. "I think maybe he slipped and fell in a small glacial fissure," he said. "But because he really wasn't in shape for this race, this might have, shall we say, 'encouraged' him not to continue." The more often the runner himself repeated the story, Gilligan recalls, the deeper the crevasse became. The other problem was potentially serious: Anthony Anderson, a forty-year-old attorney from Washington, was coming down off the glacier on the second loop of the course when he fell into a stream. He was soaked and shivering. "I was about a half mile from an aid station," Anderson said later. "When someone asked me, 'Are you OK?' I said, 'I'm not going to make it.' I decided it was more important to continue living than to finish this marathon. I know hypothermia when I see it." Indeed he did: according to Wischnia, Anderson had suffered from hypothermia in seven of his seventeen marathons to that point, suggesting that he probably would have been better off running in Atlanta than Antarctica. He was reportedly near-delirious and trembling by the time some of Gilligan's crew arrived in a four-wheel vehicle, wrapped up the runner, and carted him back to the Uruguayan base for treatment. Fortunately, he was fine by the next day.

The vast emptiness of the island was punctuated by the four research stations, and the staffs of each came out to watch and support the runners, although it was obvious that some of them really didn't understand what *support* meant in a marathon. At the Chilean base, it was later said, some runners were offered cigarettes. The Russians hoisted vodka bottles. And the Chinese waved banners and flags with colorful slogans written in their native language, which, as it later turned out, were actually advertisements inviting the runners to come and shop at their base.

One competitor decided to become a customer. Dr. Alan Turnbull, a fifty-nine-year-old surgeon from New York, walked the course, stopping to peruse the native goods for sale at the different bases and picking up various baubles and trinkets for his family and friends. "When Turnbull finished," Wischnia said, "he looked like a guy who had just completed a shopping spree on Fifth Avenue."

For most of the other eighty finishers, the effort was serious, especially the glacier, an uphill climb to the finish so severe that a few runners were reduced to scrambling along on their hands and knees. To make matters worse, a fog had rolled in, the winds had picked up, and the temperatures had dropped. Still, they persevered. Harry Johnson was the first to cross the makeshift finish line at the Uruguayan base, in a time of three hours and fourteen minutes (well over an hour slower than the winning time at a conventional marathon). Most of the others finished in times sixty to ninety minutes slower than their typical marathon finish times. Part of this was due to the long course—Gilligan later remeasured and corrected it—but another part of it was simply the almost otherworldly conditions.

"Other than climbing to the summit of Mount McKinley, this is the hardest thing I've ever done," said Cahill, the hotel mogul. "After sixteen miles, I gave up and started walking. But I was going to finish on hands and knees if that's what it took. It was a battle between me and the glacier . . . and the glacier won."

"I wasn't sure I was going to be able to finish," Churchill said. "But once I got down the glacier the second time, I thought, *We're going to make it.* It was a magical moment."

There were no complaints that afternoon as the runners, their families, and the crew had a barbecue and party out on the deck of the ships. During a champagne toast, Gilligan thanked everyone for making a little bit of running and Antarctic history. He was thankful the race had come off as well as it had, with no fatalities, no serious injuries, and no Argentine invasion. He and the other passengers sipped glasses of a lethal concoction known as an Antarctic Sunrise—a specialty of the Russian bartender on the *Ioffe*—and savored their achievement, which was far greater than running a marathon, even the toughest marathon on Earth. "We went down there and ran twenty-six miles for something more than a [finisher's] certificate," said Bernson. "We wanted to be part of something historic."

A few of the other runners, however, got to celebrate in real Antarctic style. During the marathon, an officer from the Chilean base had approached one of the race officials. "You have *women!*" he said, in awe of the female runners and spouses who were part of the event. The all-male Chilean station was in desperate need of company, particularly female. Back on the ship,

Ed and Bernadette, among others, were asked if they wanted to return to the island for a party. They were told the Chileans were very excited about this and doing a lot of work to put together an appropriately warm reception. "I thought it sounded like a great idea," Bernadette said. "After all, *I* hadn't run a marathon that day, so I was ready to go!"

About forty of the visitors—married couples and a few single women—climbed back on a couple Zodiacs and returned to King George Island. They were ushered to a small hangar, around which the lights from the helicopter landing strip had been hung. Music crackled from cheap speakers, and buckets of beer on ice sat on a table. "Welcome," said the officer, in heavily accented English. "You are in the southernmost disco in the world!" For the next two hours, the runners danced and drank and chatted with the Chileans. Although one attractive, single female marathoner was the object of much attention, and was probably asked to dance more times than she really wanted to, no one misbehaved, or at least no one that anyone can remember. "They were very friendly," Ed Sylvester recalled. Finally, at about 10:30 P.M., the ship's crew that had accompanied the group said it was time to go. The Chileans protested. "They wanted us to keep partying," Bernadette remembered. "They said, 'Just stay a couple of more hours.'"

"I thanked them," Ed recalls. "But I said, 'I just ran a marathon, I gotta go lie down.'"

The runners climbed back on the Zodiacs and slipped off into the darkening skies over Admiralty Bay. At the Chilean base on King George Island, the stereo was turned off, the lights unstrung and returned to the helicopter pad. The world's southernmost disco was closed; the first Last Marathon was over. It was, in the end, a success, by any measure. A wave of publicity would be followed by a rush of entries. The seemingly ridiculous—running 26.2 miles on some muddy, half-frozen island at the bottom of the Earth—turned out to be captivating. Why? While the race's success owed a great deal to a smart entrepreneur and a little good fortune, there was something more complex at play here. In some ways, the lure of the Antarctica Marathon is as deep as the origin of the human genus, or, others might say, as shallow as the self-absorption of one of its largest generations.

BABY, WE WERE BORN TO RUN
...BUT IN ANTARCTICA?

There has always been nobility in long-distance running. There has also been buffoonery. Not to mention myth, poetry, poison, spectacle both uplifting and appalling, and bad fashion sense.

Above all, there has been humanity.

While it may not seem so in this era of the drive-through lifestyle, long-distance running is quintessentially human. Stu Mittleman, a deep-thinking, long-distance champion who once ran solo across America, has been making this point for years. Our ability to run or walk long distances, he says, "is a gift to the human species, like language." As historical proof, he cites armies on the march, the great migrations of people across vast distances. You think 26.2 miles is a marathon? How about that one-thousand-mile trek across the frozen Bering Strait twelve thousand years ago by those who became known to us as the American Indians? Now *that* was a marathon.

In November 2004, well into the modern running boom and nine years after the first Antarctica Marathon, a major scientific study confirmed Mittleman's views while providing newspaper copy desks around the country with an almost irresistible headline slant:

HUMANS BORN TO RUN

EVEN COUCH POTATOES MAY HAVE BEEN BORN TO RUN

HUMANS NATURAL-BORN RUNNERS

The news was in reaction to the article published in the scientific journal *Nature* by two American scientists. Dr. Dennis Bramble of the University of Utah and Dr. Daniel Lieberman of Harvard University had analyzed the fossil record and concluded that early humans had evolved anatomically to run. Through that, they were able to hunt and gather foods over great distances. We started running two million years ago, they believe, and that fact, as much as our brains or opposable thumbs or anything else unique to *Homo sapiens*, is what enabled our species to survive and flourish.

"Running made us human, at least in the anatomical sense," Bramble, a specialist in biomechanics, told the *New York Times*. "We're lousy sprinters, but we're really good long-distance runners," said Lieberman, a biological anthropologist.

Early humans couldn't run as fast as other species, but we could chase our next meal until it wore itself out. The reasons for that, the researchers said, start with our long, springy tendon muscles, including the strong Achilles tendon connecting the calf muscles to the heel, and the mighty muscle of the buttocks, the gluteus maximus. All of these make humans good, natural distance runners; the "spring-loaded" tendons store and release energy, and the glutes stabilize the trunk as we move forward in the "controlled fall" of running. There are also the arches of our feet, which help give us that "spring" in our step, and the broad surface areas of our joints, to better distribute the impact forces of running (especially on the savanna of Africa, which is where early man was running). Even our upper bodies are designed for distance: Our wide shoulders are well-suited to carry the swinging arms that give us balance as we run and help propel us; our heads are held firmly in place as we run by a strong ligament. Then there are our three million sweat glands and lack of fur that help keep us cool.

Other animals lack these features; most would overheat and die after running about six miles. So it was that our prehistoric human ancestors (you could call them, on the basis of this study, our "distance" ancestors) were able to get to the food first, through what Lieberman called persistence hunting. As the name suggests, this means hunting by outlasting the prey. Because of their "built-in" advantages, our ancestors were able to stay on the trail of their prey, over long periods of time, even through the heat of the day. Essentially, this landmark study shows that we humans are nothing if not persistent and that that quality manifested itself first and foremost in our running. Other animals crawled, slithered, or sprinted for short distances. We went long—and became the dominant species.

Bramble and Lieberman's theory certainly helps explain why running feels so natural to so many people, even today. It doesn't, however, explain the urge to run a marathon in Antarctica. Neither could Lieberman himself, when posed the question in an e-mail. "I think that running evolved to allow for persistence hunting, and that is done in fairly open, remote country," the

Harvard professor wrote in his response. "A runner might go for [6.2 to 9.2 miles] or so with little company other than his thoughts and the poor animal he is chasing. So being able to run for a long time by yourself in a big open place is very normal. That said, running marathons in Antarctica is, well, a bit unusual. But so are many other things we humans do."

The idea that we were designed to run in order to live doesn't mean we were designed to run in a place where humans can't live. Also, the evidence collected by Lieberman and Bramble suggests that the persistence hunters of prehistory were running about 6 to 9 miles, not 26.2. That's a big jump in distance. How did that happen? How did we go from running 10 kilometers to 42, and for recreation not subsistence?

As society developed, man began to use his talent for distance running as a means of communication. Message runners were common in ancient (and even more modern) warfare, and commercial couriers—known as "footmen"—were widely used on the dusty roads of Europe in the sixteenth and seventeenth centuries. In the nineteenth century, competitive distance athletes, the so-called pedestrians, attracted large crowds, many of whom wagered large amounts of money on their multiday "go as you please" walking and running competitions. Still, well into the 1800s, no one aside from those who had traveled or studied Greek history had ever heard the word *marathon*. And few would think of running long distance as a kind of personal challenge. To explain the rise of the modern running and marathon movement, we must depart the realm of science for the world of words. It was not our springy tendons and glutes alone that inspired so many of us to run such prodigious lengths; the motivation sprang from the more mysterious recesses of the human character, namely our imaginations and sense of adventure.

Robert Browning was sixty-seven years old when he alloyed myth and historical fact to create a 118-line-long poem about an obscure character of Greek antiquity named Pheidippides. The eponymously titled narrative was published in 1879; but in writing it, Browning borrowed from several ancient accounts. The most important one, by the great Greek historian Herodotus, was about a professional courier who in 490 B.C. had been dispatched from Athens to Sparta to ask for assistance against an imminent Persian invasion. The messenger, named Pheidippides or Phillipides (depending on the translation), covered the 130 miles between the two cities in one day to relay his message that "the Athenians beseech you to hasten to their aid and not allow that state to be enslaved by Barbarians." The Spartans, in the midst of a feast, took their time in responding to the messenger's request. Luckily for the Athenians, they didn't need the help of their neighbors in beating the Persians on the plains of Marathon.

At the end of the battle, the later historian Plutarch wrote, two other messengers were dispatched with news of the victory. One of them, Eucles, had been wounded in the battle. Yet he managed to run (or stagger) the approximately twenty-five-mile distance from Marathon to Athens. Eucles barged into the first house he came upon, proclaimed "God save you, we are well," and dropped dead.

Browning combined the Herodotus story with the accounts of both Plutarch and yet a third chronicler, named Lucian; he then threw in a side plot about the runner's run-in with the Greek god Pan on the way to Sparta. In Browning's version it is Pheidippides who takes the message after the battle. Upon reaching not a humble house but the court of Athens, he collapses after a more pulse-pounding exit line: "Rejoice, we conquer!"

The poem "Pheidippides" appeared as part of a popular collection of Browning's work called *Dramatic Idyls*. Seventeen years later, inspired by the revived legend of Pheidippides, organizers of the first modern Olympics in Athens decided to include an event that was never part of the ancient Greek games: a 40-kilometer (24.8-mile) run from the site of the battle to the city.

They called it the "Marathon."

At this point, one must also stop and wonder just what would have happened if the legendary battle had been fought not on those heroic-sounding plains but instead through the streets of Thessaloníki, on the peninsula of Khalkidhikí, or on the island of Astypalaia. Imagine telling your friends that you were training to run the New York Khalkidhikí.

Fortunately, *Marathon* it was. And it was a hit right from the start: that first Olympic Marathon in Greece in 1898—won fittingly enough by a Greek, Spiridon Louis—sparked a marathon boom of its own. Most notably, a group of American athletes and officials from the Boston Athletic Association who had attended the 1896 Games and watched the inspiring finish by the obscure Greek shepherd came back home with the idea of starting their own long-distance race. Giving credit to the race in Greece that had given them the idea, they called their event, held for the first time in April 1897, the Boston Marathon.

Marathons soon sprouted up around the Northeast. None of those who competed in them did so for reasons that would today be considered "physical fitness." Quite the contrary. "The appeal of long-distance running centered on its danger," wrote Boston Marathon historian Tom Derderian. There was plenty of that, especially considering the preparations taken by the competitors. "Many marathoners of the early 20th century trained lightly and had little regard for even pacing," wrote Edward Sears in his book *Running Through the Ages*. "As a result, several of these early races were filled with drama and uncertainty as runners collapsed or were forced to withdraw at various stages of the race." The event itself almost seemed headed for a premature collapse: In the 1900 Olympic Marathon, finishers accused the winner of taking shortcuts through the streets of Paris. And in St. Louis in August 1904, the marathon provided a controversial finish to an Olympics so badly organized that the entire Olympics movement was almost abandoned, just eight years after it had started.

It's one of the more bizarre if forgotten races in the annals of distance running, and it's a story worth retelling, since it almost makes the Antarctica Marathon sound, by comparison, like an easy jog on a cool morning.

The 1904 race began at 3 P.M., about the hottest point of the day. Starting with five laps around the cinder track at Washington University, the thirty-one runners ran off into the stultifying St. Louis afternoon. They were preceded by a group of horsemen and a small caravan of automobiles, carrying the runners' handlers (coaches), journalists, race officials, and police. The cars, driving on already dry roads, kicked up a constant cloud of dust that settled on the pack of runners behind them. This, the heat, and a lack of water along the course (there was only one source of water, a well twelve miles from the start) led to predictable results. One competitor began vomiting after ten miles and had to quit. Another nearly choked to death from the dust. There were additional hazards: One runner was chased a mile off course by a dog.

(He eventually got back and finished ninth.) The close proximity of the automobiles also was dangerous; at one point one of the cars had to swerve to avoid hitting a competitor, and it went down an embankment. The accident severely injured two officials. Meanwhile, in the Olympic stadium, spectators and officials, including President Theodore Roosevelt's eldest daughter, twenty-year-old Alice, waited for the winner. At about three hours and thirteen minutes after the start, he appeared—or so they thought. Frederick Lorz of New York City, who had finished fifth at Boston that year, accepted the cheers of the crowd and crossed the line. "The officials bustled around and Alice Roosevelt was all ready to hand him the prize," wrote John Kieran and Arthur Daley in their 1936 book *The Story of the Olympic Games*, "when somebody called an indignant halt to the proceedings with the charge that Lorz was an impostor."

Claiming the whole thing was a joke, Lorz readily admitted that he had not run the entire race. Exhausted after nine miles, he had accepted a ride in his manager's car and rode it until about nineteen miles, when it broke down. Rather than stand around waiting for repairs, Lorz said, he figured he might as well keep running—and did so, right across the finish line.

Lorz was disqualified, and the second-place finisher, Thomas Hicks, an Englishman living in Cambridge, Massachusetts, was declared the winner. But as Alice Roosevelt waited to repeat the medal ceremony with the real winner, Hicks collapsed. It turned out to be something more than the heat that rendered him unable to stand. From about mile ten on, Hicks's handler had given him regular doses of strychnine, brandy, and egg white—a sort of "performance-enhancing" cocktail (the strychnine was believed to be a stimulant).

Supposedly, it took four doctors to revive Hicks. Reviving the modern marathon movement took four more years.

After the debacle in St. Louis, there was serious talk about banning the marathon, but it stayed on the Olympic program. The 1908 Olympic Marathon in London—one of the most important marathons ever held—sparked new interest in the race and helped seal its place as among the most heroic of human athletic endeavors. It also established the modern distance of 26.2 miles and featured one more spectacular and controversial finish. The Italian Dorando Pietri staggered into the stadium in the lead, but also in trouble. "To the horror of the crowd of 70,000, [he] wobbled in the wrong direction and collapsed," wrote Sears. "Doctors and officials rushed to the little Italian, dragged him to his feet, and started him off around the track in the proper direction." Captured on black-and-white film, the scene appears almost comical when viewed today; the diminutive mustachioed Pietri seems an almost Chaplinesque figure as he teeters along the track; the gaggle of officials surrounding him, arms waving, look like the Keystone Cops. It wasn't funny at the time, however. He was carried off on a stretcher, and rumors spread that he had died. Meanwhile, a department store clerk from New York named Johnny Hayes finished thirty seconds after Pietri had been escorted across the finish line. At first Pietri was declared the winner. The Americans, quite rightly, protested, saying that the Italian had been given illegal assistance. "An hour later, to the dismay of the emotional thousands, Pietri was disqualified and the gold medal awarded to Hayes," Sears writes. Happily, Pietri, who won the hearts of the world for his valiant efforts in London, lived to run more marathons.

Hayes was the last American to win the Olympic Marathon until Frank Shorter in 1972. The cultural impact of the latter marathon was even greater.

While Shorter's victory helped spark the running boom of the 1970s, it's important to understand the context in Munich. Shorter's victory took place at a time when more Americans, particularly professional men, were beginning to feel the urge to use their bodies in the way that (as we have seen) nature intended them to be used. There was encouragement from many corners to shake off sedentary ways, to get up, and to get moving—from President John F. Kennedy, who reenergized the President's Council on Physical Fitness to help improve the condition of both children and adults in the early 1960s, to Dr. Ken Cooper, whose book *Aerobics* in 1968 both coined a word and provided a bestselling call to action.

After Shorter's win, running looked like an exciting and noble way to do that, not to mention that it was easily available and didn't require a bicycle, a pool, or a gym. And in road racing, while you were exercising your heart you could exercise your competitive spirit as well. In the years following Shorter's victory, the morning, lunchtime, and after-work roads of America began to fill with mostly white, mostly professional, competitive, type A men. They clad themselves in garish track suits or tight short shorts and wore on their feet new-fangled "running shoes," many of them bearing the then-unfamiliar logo of a company that acknowledged the Greek tradition of running in its name (Nike was the goddess representing triumph or victory). Still, no one in those early years of the running boom was looking to run in unusual places around the world. As was the case with Gilligan and his mates on the Greater Boston Track Club, the emphasis was on competition. More miles, more races, faster times. That's what runners did (and the more who did it, the more who got hurt, which indirectly led to cross training and, later, helped spark the emergence of the triathlon as a popular participatory sport).

Very soon, many of these running boomers had quickly graduated from thirty- or forty-minute jogs around the neighborhood to the marathon. This makes sense: When you think about it, despite its Greek roots, the marathon is a very American endeavor. It's exercise to excess, taking something good—a five-mile run for fitness—and blowing it up into a 26.2-mile endurance epic. A wave of new races rolled in, most notably the New York City Marathon, which over the course of six years went from 127 "nuts" running loops around Central Park in 1970 (only 55 of them finished) to a five-borough extravaganza, attracting 2,000 runners in 1976 and almost 10,000 by 1978. Major 26.2-mile events in Chicago, Washington, D.C., and other large cities also built up steam.

In the 1990s a new marathon movement began, this one inspired not by a slight, Yale-educated lawyer with the lungs of a giant but a charismatic, African American talk show host with a weight issue and a huge national following. When a svelte Oprah Winfrey ran the 1994 Marine Corps Marathon in Washington, D.C., she inspired new thousands to take to the roads. These so-called second-generation marathon runners were predominantly women, and they had their own goals. They were running to complete, not to compete, and cared less about fast times than they did about the self-satisfaction that came with simply crossing the finish line. (Not incidentally, they also trained more intelligently for the long haul, minimizing the training miles and putting more emphasis on cross-training activities, such as weight training, bicycling, swimming, and yoga.) They also ran to raise funds for worthy causes. Because most never had a hope of winning a medal or even running fast, some decided to track their progress in other ways, by becoming marathon "collectors," running a marathon in every state or in various countries and continents around the world.

Many, observes Ryan Lamppa, who follows trends in the sport for Running USA in Santa Barbara, California, were simply looking for something new, what he calls the "hey that sounds cool" junkies. "For some, the typical large road races became 'been there, done that,'" Lamppa says. Races like the Antarctica Marathon "offered a unique way to experience running, because they're so out of the ordinary and exotic. It's kind of a badge of honor for some runners to be part of these kinds of non-traditional races." Hugh Jones of the Association of International Marathons agrees that the emergence of exotic marathons, from Antarctica to the Sahara desert, reflects a restless energy and a desire on the part of many runners to keep pushing boundaries further and further. But it's also simply an interesting way to see interesting places. "Even where there are no locals to meet, as in Antarctica," he says, "running a marathon still provides form and purpose to the trip beyond that of simply going there."

That motivation was evident in the reaction to news of the first marathon in Antarctica. Marathon Tours was flooded with requests by runners interested in doing the "next" one. Gilligan, who had never been certain there would be a next one, decided to hold a second Last Marathon, although given the logistics involved, he figured he'd need two years to organize another edition.

Those who wanted to run in his marathon and other "extreme" adventure races like it were more than thrill seekers, however. In one sense they were living out a predestination that is more human, if slightly less comfortable, than sitting in front of a steering wheel or a TV set. While we no longer needed our springy tendons to stay alive, our born-to-run advantages had become, in modern parlance, "repurposed" to provide for something just as intrinsically human: the desire to move, explore, and strike out for new horizons.

ALL FEET ON DECK

Rita Clark is from Green Bay, Wisconsin. She's not a football fan, however. She never giggled and swooned over the sight of Brett Favre at the supermarket, and she hates being called a Cheese-head. Clark does love to run, though, and at age forty-six was already experienced when she heard about the first marathon in Antarctica. *Man, oh man, that would be the ultimate place to run*, she thought.

Clark managed to register for the second edition of the race before it sold out. Thanks in part to the massive publicity generated by the first race—a front-page story in the *Wall Street Journal*, a feature in *Time*, network TV segments, and, oh yes, another big story in *Travel Agent* magazine—response was overwhelming for the second edition of the race, in February 1997. Once again, a reporter from a major magazine came along. This time, it was John Walters from *Sports Illustrated*.

There would be plenty of good material for him.

Assembled on board the two ships was what would soon become recognized as the ordinary cast of extraordinary characters for this trip: Guys who had climbed Mount Everest. Grizzled outdoorsmen and women who had trekked to the North Pole. Runners who had completed hundreds of marathons. Amazing comeback stories, like Pat Rummerfield, a forty-four-year-old who had been paralyzed in a car crash back in 1974. Fourteen years later, he rose and walked. Eventually, he completed an Ironman triathlon. Now, he was in Antarctica. "I'm a walking miracle," he told Walters.

Some very good runners also made the trip, such as Scott Dvorak, a five-thousand-meter runner in the 1996 U.S. Olympic Trials, and Michael Collins of Ireland, who had finished third in his country's marathon championships. Despite runners with such serious credentials, Clark remembers the voyage there being low-key, a lot of fun. "Good food, partying in the bar," she says. "We had a great time." Except for those who suffered from seasickness, a common ailment on the rough waters of the Drake Passage. One newlywed couple spent most of their time in their cabin. "Unfortunately," Clark says, "it was because they were sick."

The weather affected this marathon more than the first. On race day a sudden surge of ten-foot-high ocean swells prevented the *Ioffe* from landing its runners, unaware that the *Vavilov* had already managed to do so earlier. Andrew Prossin, the Canadian expedition leader who would serve the same role on future Antarctica Marathon trips, convened the *Ioffe*'s forty-three runners in the mess hall. "Conditions are borderline," he said. "But considering the importance of this event, we're going to go ahead and try to get you ashore." At this point, as the ship rocked and the winds howled, Dvorak leaned over to Walters and whispered, "I think I speak for everyone when I say, it isn't *that* important."

As it turned out, others would disagree. On King George Island, the runners from the other ship got tired of waiting and begged Gilligan to start the race. He finally relented. In what would become, in effect, the Last Marathon II-A, Collins and Ray Brown crossed the finish line together in a superb time of 2:33:49. By the time they'd finished, the *Ioffe* runners had arrived, and were soon set off on the second race of the day. This one was won by Dvorak, in an even faster time—2:23:11. It was, he later told writer Kimi Puntillo, "the toughest course I ever ran."

Controversy erupted over who would be named the winner of the 1997 Last Marathon. According to Walters's account in *Sports Illustrated*, Collins and Brown wanted to be named co-winners, along with Dvorak, even though their times on the same course were slower. "What's the big deal?" Gilligan said. "This isn't even a certified race." But it was indeed a big deal to the two gentlemen, and Gilligan relented. The next day, in a ceremony on the deck of the *Vavilov*, Gilligan honored Dvorak, Collins, and Brown as "our top three finishers." Rita Clark heard the scuttlebutt at the awards ceremony. Like many of those on board, she said, she wondered what the fuss was about. "We're all competitive," she said. "But, it's not like there was prize money. Like [Gilligan] said, it wasn't a real sanctioned event. If you really wanted a competitive race, I think you needed to run somewhere else other than Antarctica."

For Clark the 1997 race wasn't about the controversy over who actually won. It was the sight of one of the skuas flying off with a flag that marked the course and left her running aimlessly for a while. It was one of the scientists manning an aid station, who said to her, in a thick Spanish accent, "You look tired . . . you stop . . . you rest." She said, "I can't stop, I'm running a race!" And then there was the guy from Minnesota who wore only a T-shirt and shorts on race day despite the 30-degree temperatures. He loved needling Clark about being a Cheesehead from Green Bay. One day they spotted a blue iceberg that looked for all the world like a colossal slice of cheese. "There's the iceberg for you, Cheesehead," the Minnesotan cried out, eliciting a wave of laughter on the ship.

Antarctica had a lasting effect on Clark, and not necessarily in the deep spiritual or philosophical way it did on many others. The day after the marathon, the ship visited another one of the South Shetland Islands. They climbed to the top of a large hill, and while most enjoyed the view before gingerly descending, a few, including Clark, decided it would be much more fun to slide back down: "butt skiing," they called it. "It was like a ride at a big fair," she said. "You'd slide down, and at some points you'd go so fast you were airborne." She had so much fun "butt skiing" that when she returned to Green Bay, she decided to take up the luge. Clark also returned to her longtime passion, volunteer work with young girls. Her efforts apparently met with sufficient distinction to earn a Community Service Award—bestowed on her by the Green Bay Packers.

Though going to Antarctica was not part of Clark's volunteer efforts, by the time of the 1999 Last Marathon a new trend had emerged in road running. More and more men and women were running marathons to help raise funds for charity. The thinking went like this: People want the sense of fulfillment and accomplishment that comes with running a marathon. The charitable organization would help them do that by giving these people training opportunities and paying for their travel to a marathon. In return, the runners would each raise a few thousand dollars for the charity. This appeal to both self-interest and altruism was pioneered by the Leukemia & Lymphoma Society—whose Team in Training became a major force in the marathon world—and adopted by other not-for-profit organizations, including Memorial Sloan-Kettering Cancer Center in New York City. Named after Fred Lebow, the New York City Marathon founder who had died of brain cancer in 1994, "Fred's Team" had a great appeal to another, less-famous Fred.

When Fred Lipsky's father was diagnosed with prostate cancer, he decided to run a marathon for Sloan-Kettering. "I figured I'd do a *mitzvah* . . . a good deed," said Lipsky, a police officer in suburban Suffolk County, New York. To raise money for his race, the 1996 New York City Marathon, Lipsky sent out flyers throughout his precinct. Money poured in. Within a week, he had made the one thousand dollars then needed to join Fred's Team. Along with the checks and cash came letters and cards congratulating him for his efforts.

Lipsky was amazed at the response to his fundraising efforts and thoroughly enjoyed the marathon experience—especially, he jokes, the post-race beers. So after New York, he decided to do another fundraising marathon: Dublin in fall 1997. When he got there, he saw a lanky fellow wearing a striking Last Marathon/Antarctica jacket. Lipsky went over to the guy and asked him if he had run the race. "We organized it," the man replied. His name was Cliff Jennings, another Long Islander who had become Thom Gilligan's right-hand man at Marathon Tours. Jennings had been on the 1997 trip and told Lipsky about the journey, the ship, the penguins, the icebergs, the race, and the awesome power of Antarctica. The cop was won over. "I knew there'd be a lot of wacky people on that trip, so I'd fit right in," he said.

There were—including the three college students that Lipsky, then forty-one, had befriended while the runners were still in Ushuaia, at the tip of Argentina, prior to boarding the ships for the passage to Antarctica in February 1999. Antsy to get a taste of what they thought they might experience on the Last Continent, he and the three students hiked up a mountain behind their hotel. They clambered higher and higher, over several ridges, up and around loose rocks. "Suddenly," Lipsky recalls, "we're in snow up to our chests." The kids pressed on a little further, but they eventually decided it was time to head back. As they gingerly descended the slope after their impromptu adventure, Lipsky realized how all four of them could have disappeared into a crevasse, and no one would have had any idea what had happened to them. "I'm the cop, I'm supposed to be the responsible one," he said to himself. "What was I thinking?"

After a harrowing trip across the passage—forty-foot waves rocked the ships and shook even the cop's cool as he hung on his bunk rails for dear life—they arrived on King George Island for the marathon. Soon enough, Lipsky found himself again clambering up the slope of the glacier. "They said it was about a mile," he said. "It felt like a thousand." In the warm (low thirties) temperatures, he found himself sinking into the slushy ice—at one point he was up to his knees and had to stop and extricate his leg with both hands. When you have to extricate your leg from anything in the middle of a marathon, something is amiss. At that point, Lipsky realized he needed an Antarctic attitude adjustment, immediately. "You can't look at the Antarctica Marathon as a competitive race," he says now, looking back. "You have to look at it as a fast-paced day hike without backpacks, or just a kind of crazy adventure. But you can't think of it as a race." Despite the conditions, Lipsky was tenth out of 113 finishers, running a fine Antarctic time of three hours and forty-five minutes. The race was a success in another way, since he raised twenty-four thousand dollars for Sloan-Kettering. "I was lucky," he said. "I did my good deed and got to go on the trip of a lifetime."

Those in the next edition of the race, in 2001, might not have counted themselves as lucky, but they did get to participate in one of the most bizarre foot races ever staged and certainly the most talked-about, controversial edition of the marathon in Antarctica.

By this point, the Last Marathon had become one of the hottest tickets in adventure travel. To simplify the logistics, Gilligan had confined the trip to just one of Marine Expeditions' ships: the *Lyubov Orlova*, named after a glamorous Russian movie star of the 1930s. (Pictures of her were hung throughout the ship.) A 331-foot-long research vessel designed to plow through ice three feet thick, the *Lyubov Orlova* was reconverted for the marathon in a way that Gilligan described as "spartan, but comfortable." On board were 140 passengers. The median age was forty-five, although one runner, Jules Winkler, a widower and retired jeweler—also from Long Island—was seventy-one.

A barrel-chested, gravelly voiced navy veteran, Winkler would become one of the unique characters in the annals of the Antarctica Marathon. Larry Davidson, who coached Winkler through his first marathon in 1999, quoted the author F. Scott Fitzgerald in describing the elder runner. "You know [Fitzgerald's] line that 'there are no second acts in American life?'" Davidson says. "For Jules that's how I look at it. He had a second act because of his involvement in running."

That involvement came at a dark point for Winkler. In late 1997, Phyllis, his wife of forty-three years, was diagnosed with pancreatic cancer. Seven months later, on April 1, 1998, she died. "That was a devastating thing for me," Winkler recalls. "My wife didn't die easily. It was a very agonizing death." Five days after his wife's passing, a grief-stricken Winkler received a flyer in the mail advertising Team in Training, the then-new fundraising program for the Leukemia & Lymphoma Society. It was the Leukemia Society that had developed the template for marathon fundraising and would eventually become, by far, the biggest and most successful of the various programs.

RUN A MARATHON . . . IN RETURN, YOU'LL HELP SAVE A LIFE was the headline of the brochure.

Winkler gulped hard and thought about Phyllis. "It really hit me . . . this was something I ought to get into in her memory."

Winkler was no stranger to exercise or hard work at that point. Born in the Bronx, he had learned the jeweler's trade from his father and worked in the Diamond District of midtown Manhattan. There, he would painstakingly shape and set diamonds for his clients—million dollar jobs, some of them, including a diamond-studded watch for then-president Dwight Eisenhower. In the late 1950s he and Phyllis moved out to Hicksville, on suburban Long Island, where they raised two children, Rick and Donna. An avid physical fitness buff, Winkler would rise at 4:45 every morning, catch an early train to the city, and head to the YMCA on Twenty-Third Street, where he would lift weights and run the indoor track before starting work. He eventually got into marathon running and in 1977 finished the New York City Marathon in a time of three hours and fifty-nine minutes—his best time at the 26.2 mile distance.

By the time Team in Training came calling, all that was almost twenty-five years in the past. Standing on the threshold of a new and potentially bleak, lonely phase of his life—his wife gone, kids grown—Winkler decided to learn the sport afresh, this time as part of a group of runners coached by Davidson and sponsored by Team in Training. Through spring 1999 they trained for a marathon in Anchorage, Alaska. Along with his new training partners, Winkler decided to adopt a new philosophy to running. "When I was younger," he said, "I was pushing hard all the time. Now I said to myself, *If I want to keep running marathons, I'm just going to run them to finish.*"

As part of his involvement with the Team in Training program, Winkler had to raise money for the Leukemia Society—which he did by writing all his friends and family and asking them in turn to send an appeal to fifteen of their friends as well. His chain letter strategy worked. "I needed to raise $4,000," he recalls. "I got $12,000."

The group traveled to Alaska together in June 1999. All finished the race. While in Anchorage, Winkler heard other runners talking about their quests to run other 26.2 mile races in various places around the world. "That's when I started to think about getting seven continents," he recalled. "I thought it would be cool to make this a goal."

So it was that Winkler found himself in Ushuaia in February 2001, about to board the *Lyubov Orlova*. It had been many years since Winkler had set foot on a ship, and he had heard all the horror stories about upchucking in the Drake Passage. But the first day on board the ship, the affable Winkler—who attracted attention as the oldest runner on the trip—picked up a valuable tip from one of the Russian crewmen who spoke English. It was just prior to embarking. Winkler was wandering around the dock area in Ushuaia when he heard the Russian crewman speaking to someone in broken English. "Hey, is it a rough trip to Antarctica?" Winkler asked the man.

"Very rough," replied the sailor. "But I give you little secret. Did you eat today?"

"Yeah," Winkler replied. "I had a big lunch in town."

"Good," he said. "Eat dinner, too. Eat big dinner on ship. And keep eating."

The man went on to explain that keeping a full stomach was one way to keep from getting seasickness. "It had something to do with the acid in your stomach," Winkler said. "I didn't really care about the science behind it. If this guy—a Russian sailor who'd been back and forth to Antarctica a dozen times—told me it worked, then I was all for it."

So Winkler followed his advice: food and plenty of fresh air. Both were in plentiful supply. The food on the trip was "excellent," and the fresh air was just a few steps away, out on the deck. "That's what I did all the way to Antarctica. I ate and stood out on the deck, enjoying myself, while everybody else was throwing up."

Once they arrived in the calmer waters of Antarctica, the vomiting stopped and the sight-seeing began: penguin rookeries, seal colonies, icebergs. At night, there were lectures, discussions, and amusing and sometimes tipsy interactions between the runners and the Russian crew. "They like the runners," said Gilligan. "Generally, people going to Antarctica are bird-watchers or scientific types. Here, we're a group of high-energy passengers who were really interested in seeing everything and doing everything."

That pent-up energy was ready to be released on February 8, the day of the 2001 race. The ship anchored off King George

Island. But that morning, weather conditions deteriorated. There was a forty-mile-per-hour wind and six-foot-high waves. Too dangerous, the captain said, to attempt to land the Zodiacs. The runners were disappointed, but they had no choice. "You don't argue with the captain," said Gilligan. "Out there, his word is law." The next day, conditions were still bad. The ship weighed anchor, and the runners went off on some sight-seeing excursions. They returned to King George that night, hopeful that weather conditions for the next day—the last in their four-day window—would be better. They weren't. The ship's captain again determined conditions were too difficult to attempt a landing. That meant no marathon. "There was almost a riot," Winkler recalled. "These people had paid a lot of money to come all the way here to run a marathon. Now they were being told they couldn't." As he recalled it, passengers were arguing, pleading, offering to sign waivers releasing the tour operators from any responsibility . . . anything, if they would just please, please let them run. No dice. At that point, Winkler recalls, "I just mentioned to someone, 'Why don't we run it on the ship?'"

While some of the passengers laughed, others continued to plead with Gilligan, who ended the meeting by saying he would see what he could do. The crowd dispersed; Winkler went back to his cabin to take a nap. An hour later, Gilligan reassembled the runners with a proposed solution: The passengers had come to run a marathon. Well, run a marathon they would . . . on the deck of the ship. Quickly, a 26.2-mile course was measured out and calculated: 422 laps. "We had no alternative," said Gilligan. "There was no place in Antarctica where we could just show up and hold a marathon."

Winkler, in his cabin, woke up to the sound of feet clomping down the gangway outside his porthole. "What the hell is going on?" he called out. "We're running the marathon on the ship" was the reply. Regardless of who came up with the idea, Winkler said, he was ready to make like a gerbil in a frigid cage. "As I was doing it," Winkler says, "I was thinking, *This isn't a physical challenge, it's a mental challenge.*"

Over the next twenty-four hours, running in three shifts—afternoon, midnight, and the following morning—a total of 108 runners completed the 26.2-mile marathon around the ship. There was a high number of bruised arms, scraped elbows, and cut foreheads from runners banging into parts of the ship's superstructure as they jogged around the deck, funneling through a single door at one point. Marathoners who run out of energy talk about "hitting the wall." Here the term took on literal meaning. "I hit the wall five times," joked the first finisher, Mark Kalla. "I hit that overhead beam on the doorway and knocked myself down five times." Winkler ended up with a gash on his shoulder, from repeatedly smashing into the door.

As the competitors continued smashing their way through the impromptu marathon, the ship slowly made its way to the sheltered and magnificent Neko Harbor, on the Antarctic Peninsula. Marc Chalufour would later describe it this way for *Running Times* magazine:

> Anchored in the corner of the Harbor, the *Orlova* was dwarfed by the glaciers, each separated from the next by the jagged peak of a mountain which towered over the water. The occasional thundering crackle of the ice calving reverberated around the harbor, and by mid-afternoon the ship was surrounded by chunks of ice recently freed from the glaciers that had been ceaselessly pushing towards

the coast for thousands of years. Seals sunned themselves on the flattest of these bergs, while penguins flitted in and out of the water, and a dozen whales swam leisurely in the mouth of the harbor.

Given the surroundings, maybe running 422 laps around the deck of a ship wasn't so bad after all. By the end of the day, the mood was festive again. There were more side trips, more lectures and presentations, and more partying. The last night on board, recrossing the Drake, there were toasts to the first marathon ever held on a ship. "We didn't get to run on a glacier, but we did something nobody ever did," said Winkler. "And we still got to go to Antarctica, which few people do."

The story of the 2001 Antarctica Marathon was widely reported in mainstream media around the United States, confirming again the lengths to which runners would go to compete in the Last Continent—or at least on a ship in the Last Continent. It soon became a legend in the running community, and to those outside, another example of the apparent insanity of marathon runners. Winkler went on to become a coach for Team in Training and continued running, all over the country and internationally (he is also happily remarried). Yet, he says, no matter where he is—London, Alaska, Egypt, Australia, or just out on the bike path near his home—when the marathon in Antarctica comes up in conversation, someone will inevitably say, "Hey, isn't that the one where they ran the whole thing on the ship?'" Winkler will beam and tell them that he was there. "I'm not an elite runner," he says. "I haven't won many awards in my life. But I'm proud that I ran that marathon on the ship in Antarctica. I think we're part of a little chapter in running history."

Going South

I wasn't ready to run laps around a ship, but as 2005 drew near, I was ready for Antarctica, a fiftieth-birthday, midlife-crisis adventure to beat the band.

Final instructions arrived from Marathon Tours not long after Christmas. We were encouraged to purchase special traveler's insurance—I presume this was the "in case of being sucked into the Southern Ocean or dying of overexposure on an ice floe" policy—and to take certain items. The packing list, with its accompanying text, seemed designed to question our sanity at having even gotten involved in this.

- One large duffel bag or pack; "hard luggage is impractical since it cannot be folded and stored in your cabin."
- A trail shoe with good support and traction, "since some of the run might be in an inch or two of snow. Bring two pair so that you can make a change after the first loop if your shoes are wet and muddy."

- Rain gear or waterproof outerwear, because "you will get hit with spray while in the Zodiacs in some landings."
- Rubber boots (three asterisks next to this item): "You must have a pair of knee high rubber boots since you will constantly be stepping into a foot of water. They are also appropriate for walking in mud and penguin dung. Home Depot has inexpensive ones that are perfect."

Was I signing up to run a marathon in Antarctica or become a plumber's assistant? I figured I could probably start by going down to Home Depot and looking for these boots in the Penguin Dung section. Meanwhile, we also needed to plan what to wear for the race. Marathon Tours recommended a Gore-Tex suit outer layer over polypropylene tights, a long-sleeve top—made, as most winter running fabrics now are, with a "wicking" fabric, which removes moisture from the skin to keep you dry—lightweight running gloves, and a hat. A lot of gear, in what is usually a pretty inexpensive sport, not to mention the five-thousand-dollar cost of the trip. This was adding up.

Of course, I was not alone in complaining about expenses. Travel to Antarctica has never been inexpensive, and those making the trip have rarely felt inclined to pay for it out of their own pocket. Prior to setting sail for their ill-fated 1911–12 expedition, Teddy Evans, Captain Scott's second in command, fretted over the supplies he needed to get the *Terra Nova* shipshape and provisioned. There were, he commented wryly, "a multitude of necessities to be thought of, selected, and not paid for if we could help it." That's the old Antarctic spirit! And while my shopping list paled when compared with Captain Evans's, I decided to borrow one of his era's ideas. His boss, Scott; his rivals Shackleton and

Amundsen; and presumably every other late-nineteenth- and early-twentieth-century explorer worth his pith helmet or dog sled were forever gallivanting about trying to raise money for their expeditions. For the most part these guys were not funded by their governments. They had to go out and raise money as if they were a charity, a private college, or a political candidate. "Yet another begging campaign," grumbled Scott, before heading off on one more fundraising tour in 1911.

At that time, the money was typically raised through lectures, dinners, or "subscriptions" forked over by wealthy backers or organizations such as the Royal Geographical Society. Today, of course, it would have been different. Amundsen, Scott, and Shackleton would have slick fundraising operations, including Web sites and brochures, befitting their own personal styles. Amundsen, the endurance athlete, might have sponsored a series of "Run with Roald" fundraising 5Ks; the personable Shackleton would have been slapping backs and pocketing checks over cocktails at swank country clubs. And Scott, a "quiet, withdrawn" man according to one biographer, would have stayed home and used his formidable writing talents to dash off irresistible direct-mail solicitation letters, unknown in his day but the kind we are all routinely bombarded with now. ("You and I can make history together! With your help, I can stand on the South Pole, and you will stand beside me, in spirit. And, if you act now, you'll get absolutely free this limited-edition 'Great Scott, We Did It!' coffee mug . . .")

In the early 1900s, however, they didn't have the sophisticated techniques of what is today called "development" or "direct marketing." So in addition to the dinners and societies, they resorted to a time-honored method of raising cash: they hit up their friends and family. I decided to follow in the fine tradition of getting other people to pay for my adventure, although I wouldn't exactly tell them that's what they were paying for. I would set up a series of events, ostensibly for my fiftieth birthday—January 27, 2005, exactly twenty-five days before the marathon. My friends would come and bring presents, most of which could be used for the trip or traded back in for stuff I needed for the trip.

The plan worked beautifully. The weekend of my birthday, I invited my entire training group out for a run, followed by breakfast. It was a bitter January morning, below twenty degrees and windy. ("Is this what it's going to be like in Antarctica?" someone asked. "Oh, no," I replied with grim assurance. "It'll be much worse.") Still, about a dozen of my friends turned out to do all or part of the fifteen-mile run, and, more important, all bore gifts. That night we had a birthday dinner in a swank local restaurant. My mom and my father-in-law hosted it (that my wife has the same birthday, although we're a year apart, helped here). We had about three dozen friends and family attend—more presents. After dropping numerous hints, another circle of friends finally decided to shut me up by throwing a dinner the following Saturday night, at our favorite Japanese restaurant. I was showered with sushi and still more gifts.

After the last fundraising . . . er, birthday . . . event, I counted up my take. There were a few items of running apparel that I didn't need, but these could be easily traded in for stuff I did; gift cards to local outdoor and sporting good stores, an all-purpose gift card or two, and—big score—somebody bought me luggage. It was a hard suitcase, perfect for a business trip to Chicago but no good for stashing under the bunk of a Russian expedition ship. However, it was expensive, which meant I could swap it for that gigantic duffel bag on the packing list. The only thing missing was a gift coupon to Home Depot. *Well, I'll have to break down and buy those boots myself.*

Now came the provisioning of my little expedition. Armed with gift cards, unwanted merchandise, and receipts, I headed to the shopping mall. The trip was planned with the precision of a commando raid—I'd go on a weekday, during off-hours, when they least expected me, and I worked out in advance which stores I would hit, and with which gift cards. It went like clockwork. First, the outdoor store, where I bought a pair of Gore-Tex gloves that looked thick enough to handle toxic chemicals. Then, the luggage store, for a duffel bag that unfolded to about the size of my living room ("Can I have a bag for it?" I joked at the checkout counter. The gray-haired salesman just furrowed his brow, having no doubt heard that joke several hundred times before). Next was the sporting goods store for a couple of pairs of extra-thick Thor-lo socks and a pair of cool-looking UV-protected sunglasses, and finally the book store—yes, given the amount of time we'd be spending on planes and boats, I knew I needed good reading material. I bought David Thomson's excellent book *Scott, Shackleton, and Amundsen: Ambition and Tragedy in the Antarctic* and, for light reading, a thick paperback novel by Bernard Cornwell about a merry band of sadistic medieval archers.

I still had a few more trips to make, including one not covered by gift cards.

The last thing I wanted was to get seasick on the way to Antarctica, and from what I had heard about the previous editions of the race, many had. My ear doctor, Dr. Shain Schley, a soft-spoken, gentlemanly southerner with a practice in Manhattan, gave me a brief tutorial on the problem. He explained how motion sickness is brought on by a disconnect between what you see and what your balance organs sense. Although the majority of adults don't suffer from it, he added ominously, most people will get sea-sick "if the stimulation is strong enough." (At that moment, I flashed back to Lipsky's story about forty-foot waves on the Drake Passage.) What about the eating tip I'd heard about from Jules Winkler? Dr. Schley shrugged. "You're runnin' a marathon," he drawled, "so you should be eatin' anyway." Hard to argue with that advice. I did get a prescription for a patch, a popular method of preventing motion sickness that involves placing behind your ear, eight hours before you go to sea, an adhesive patch that slowly releases into your body an anti-seasickness drug called scopolamine. My brother Chris, a sport fisherman, had a simpler and more traditional solution: "Get out on the deck if you feel sick," he said. Breathing some fresh air and seeing the horizon steady, he explained, helps with the feeling of imbalance that is part of the motion sickness problem.

Now it was time to hit the running specialty stores. One of them, the Runner's Edge, is in my town, and over lunch I had told its owner, Bob Cook, what I was planning. He thought the whole idea was splendid and said he wanted to give me a fiftieth birth-day/bon voyage gift: an entire running outfit. We spent a half-hour in his store, a few weeks before leaving, as he guided me through racks of what he called base layers and outer shells. What I really cared about was how the outfit looked and how it felt. I walked out of the store with a pair of Hind loose-fitting polypropylene running pants and a zippered blue-and-black Craft top, plus a thin, long-sleeve "base layer" (fancy endurance-apparel talk for an undershirt) that felt as soft as lambskin. Last but not least, a ski band to wear around my head, with a Runner's Edge logo on it. "Maybe that'll end up in the finish line photo," Bob chuckled. "We could use the publicity."

Next stop: New York City, to another running store. My brother and sister-in-law had given me a one-hundred-dollar gift certificate to the Super Runner Shops in Manhattan. Another friend, Mike Keohane, managed the Super Runners Shop on the East Side. Mike, who competed in the 1992 Olympic Trials Marathon, has a resting pulse of about two beats per minute, and I don't think anything fazes him—not demanding Upper West Side yuppies who come into his store, not kids who knock over entire racks of shoes, not indecisive people who want to try on sixteen pairs of shoes before they decide that maybe they don't really want a pair of running shoes after all. He takes it all in stride. So I guess it wasn't surprising that when I marched into his store and announced that I needed a pair of trail running shoes because "I'm running the Antarctica Marathon," he didn't flinch. "That's nice," he said, leading me over to a wall display of trail shoes. Slightly deflated, I tried on a few pairs and settled on a snazzy, silver-and-black pair of Saucony trail-running shoes. Water resistant, and with reinforced rubber soles to help give your feet a better grip on the soft surfaces, these were the shoes that would lead me up the glacier and to glory, I thought, as I marched out of the store.

Because you never, ever, want to run a marathon in a pair of new running shoes (no one is really sure why, but that's the advice we always go by), I ran with my Sauconys once before leaving, when my wife (Donna), son (Andrew), and I took a weekend trip in early February to New Paltz, a lovely college town and ski area located a couple hours' drive north of New York City. On a cold Sunday morning, I broke in my new shoes along a snow covered trail that followed the right-of-way of an abandoned rail line.

The Sauconys grabbed the firmly packed snow like a pair of radial tires. The trees around me were draped in snow; a breeze rustled their branches, sending soft sprays of flakes through the air. Ah, I thought, a little preview of Antarctica (forgetting that there are no trees on the entire continent). It was a wonderful, winter morning's run. Over coffee back at the hotel, I felt buoyant and upbeat. Running down there, I confidently predicted to Donna on the basis of this workout, was going to be just fine.

Time was ticking away by now; two weeks left to go. I knew that I should have done a little more trail running, to try to simulate the conditions I might meet in Antarctica, but because most of the trails where I live were long ago paved over and renamed highways, it didn't make much sense. Instead, I prepared for Antarctica in a different way: I watched it on television. It was a really cold winter in New York, and I preferred to stay indoors and run on the treadmill in the basement. While I ran along, logging my miles to nowhere, I again watched the British docudrama *The Last Place on Earth*. The series depicted Captain Robert Falcon Scott—who was practically deified in Britain after his 1912 death—as a stubborn amateur, representative not of Britain's greatness but of an empire in decline. Amundsen, by comparison, was skilled in the ways of the wild and as pure as Norwegian snow. It wasn't quite that simple. More recent biographers have pointed out that Amundsen's single-mindedness sometimes led him to dissemble and deceive in order to achieve his goals, while Scott, although he certainly made some mistakes and was very much a product of his class and his age, was also a brave, sensitive, and intelligent man. Watching, even in dramatized form, the slow death of Scott's party to exposure was far more disturbing this time around—possibly because in 1985, when I had initially watched it while training for my first marathon, I was not on the verge of going to the same part of the world in which he had perished.

Actually, what weighed on my mind more than my safety was my wife's sanity. Leaving for Antarctica in the middle of the school year was an enormous inconvenience to everyone around me. I was able to work it out with the students in my college classes, which met once a week (while I was gone, they worked independently on various projects assigned to them . . . or at least that's what they told me). But Donna was really going to have to pick up a lot of slack at home. I would have no e-mail access for the better part of two weeks; so she'd have to go through the fifty to seventy-five e-mails I routinely receive each day, delete most of them, and answer a few that couldn't wait. She'd also have to handle spirited nine-year-old Andrew without having dad around to threaten to take away his portable PlayStation when he didn't do his homework. Also, she'd be alone, except for my good-natured, eighty-three-year-old father-in-law, who could be counted on to drop by about six times a day and drive his daughter nuts.

All this excess stress and upset, I thought at one point. For what? So that I could score a few professional points . . . scratch an itch . . . impress people at the kind of cocktail parties we rarely went to anymore? Suddenly, I was beset by doubts as to my motivations. Then there was the even more important matter of my comfort. Yes, I know it may sound odd, but while running a marathon is by design an exercise in extreme discomfort, I like to be as comfortable as possible leading up to the point in the race where I feel like crap. A few years earlier, I had written a book called *The Essential Runner*, a beginner's guide to the sport. My running friends got a lot of yuks out of that. "Your next book should be *The Pampered Runner*," said my tough-girl friend Patty.

She was referring to my penchant for weekly massages, a personal trainer, chiropractors, and various physicians with whom I would make emergency appointments at the first sign of a hangnail, not to mention my carefully regimented diet and the fact that I managed to get eight or nine hours of sleep a night. The worst was when I admitted that I had gone to Chinatown in lower Manhattan and gotten a foot massage. (It was really good.)

Admittedly, I was not the roughing-it type. I wasn't even semi-rough. At the end of the day—maybe even not quite the end, maybe, say, at about noon—I was generally ready for a roof over my head and a shower. How was I going to handle ten days on a ship in Antarctica?

We'd soon find out. On February 18, I gave Andrew a really big hug and Donna a really heartfelt kiss, stuffed my gear in the trunk of an airport limo, and drove off.

▲ ▲ ▲

Lugging behind me that duffel bag, which was now stuffed to the point where it resembled a small, portable house, I checked in at the Aerolineas Argentinas counter. I had been warned about this lot. "Third World air travel," one of my globe-trotter friends sniffed. "They'll lose your luggage." That I doubted, considering the girth of my überbag. Still, I braced for snafus, miscues and delays that never came over the course of the four flights I would take with the financially struggling airline over the next two weeks. It was smooth sailing all the way—and let the record show that I made a modest contribution to those efforts on the first night of our journey.

One of the last e-mails I'd sent before leaving home was to my friend Rob, a gentle, church-going family man who also happens to be an air traffic controller at JFK International Airport. Over dinner a few months earlier, he had told me to contact him before my next international flight out of Kennedy. I wasn't quite sure what he could or couldn't do but figured he wasn't about to redirect my flight to Cleveland, so prior to leaving I sent him our flight info and promptly forgot about it.

On Friday night, February 18, I boarded a crowded Airbus 340 for the eleven-hour flight to Buenos Aires. Some people easily marked as runners were hanging around. They wore Boston Marathon jackets, Marathon Tours gear, paraphernalia from exotic events around the globe ("2000 Comrades Marathon, South Africa"; "2002 Great Wall of China Marathon") and the jogging suits that always seem inappropriate anywhere outside of a race. We settled in, taxied out on the runway, and prepared for the long wait that is the rule at JFK, especially on a Friday night. I cracked open my Bernard Cornwell book about the archers and figured it would be several chapters' worth of medieval pillaging before our wheels were even up. Just then, I felt the plane lurch and noticed that we were taxiing up the runway, passing other aircraft like flags on the United Nations Plaza: Finnair, British Air, Air France, American Airlines, all stood at attention as humble, near-bankrupt Aerolineas Argentinas rolled by. Then over the loudspeakers, in Spanish and English, the command to prepare for takeoff, and within minutes we were soaring into the night sky. "That was quick," said the woman sitting next to me. At that moment I heard my name being called, in heavily accented English, on the PA. I was being summoned to the front of the aircraft.

I stood up and felt the eyes of every passenger in the cabin on me. The woman next to me squirmed and looked around embarrassedly, as if to say, "I don't know him!" Trying to appear calm, I strode up toward the cockpit, all the while imagining an expired passport or some other unforeseen glitch that would end my Antarctica trip before it started. At the head of the first-class section, a male flight steward with a thin mustache stood, looking severe.

"Señor Hank?"

I nodded, too nervous to correct his pronunciation of my oft-mispronounced name (it's "Hance" as if there were an "e" on the end).

He smiled and produced from behind a curtain a very large and expensive-looking bottle of champagne. "The pilot, he wants to thank you for the tower."

Thank me . . . for what?

The steward searched for the words, and gestured back toward the ground. "The tower . . . your friend."

Then I realized. Rob had come through! I made a quick mental addition to my Christmas card list for the next year.

I returned to my seat, smiling sheepishly as I clutched the bottle of champagne. When I explained to the woman next to me what had happened, she managed to dilute the fine bubbly with ice water. "Humph," she sniffed. "The least they could have done is upgrade you to first class." Compared with her, the sadistic English archers sacking Caen seemed far more forgiving. I returned to my novel and stayed there.

We arrived in the morning, blinking in the sunlight and choking over the wall of humidity that hit us at the terminal. As we cleared customs, there was Thom Gilligan, looking a bit like a general marshaling his troops on the eve of battle. Except unlike a general, Gilligan was going to have to listen to every one of his

soldiers' gripes or concerns, which, I could see, surfaced immediately as a clutch of runners descended on him, some waving
forms or invoices.

Not a good time to bother him, I thought, as we climbed on
to air-conditioned buses for the ride into Buenos Aires. In that
city of three million, more than two hundred participants from
around the world would assemble and spend a few days enjoying
what is often called the Paris of South America in its high summer before heading down to Ushuaia, our jumping-off point for
Antarctica.

This was not a happy time for the enormous city that spread
out before us. Just a little over three years before, in December
2001, Argentina had defaulted on its international loans, plunging the country into a crippling depression complete with home-
lessness, riots, and frequent changes of government. As I drove
along a highway overlooking the city, blocks of elegant architec-
ture appeared next to streets lined with crumbling houses. I saw
one structure with a collapsed roof, and yet people appeared to
be living in its exposed interior.

We arrived at the Marriott hotel in the Florida section of the
city, and you would have thought we really were in Paris. The
hotel was opulent, my room dazzling in the whiteness of its cur-
tains and the softness of the king-sized bed. And for this, I probably paid the equivalent of about five dollars.

Eager to stretch my legs after the long flight, I went for a walk
with a runner I'd met on the bus. He was called Charles from
Charlestown, Massachusetts. "They named the place after me!"
he said with a grin. We ambled around the neighborhood, eventually ending up at a coffee bar at the massive Retiro railroad station. As we sipped espressos, he told me his story.

Charles Monahan was a lawyer and a naval reservist. He was also a very large guy for a runner—about 6 feet 3 inches and 250 pounds. He had played college football at Notre Dame and later coached high school and, even at age sixty-five, you got the sense he could still clobber you with one well-aimed forearm to the head. Charles was also a Vietnam veteran—he flew 238 air reconnaissance missions for the navy—and a cancer survivor; his disease, he claimed, was caused by exposure to Agent Orange, which had been used near his base outside Da Nang. He started running in 2003, after surgery and treatment, and had soon caught the marathon bug. Like many on the trip, part of his goal was to run a marathon on all seven continents. Having already completed 26.2-milers in Boston (North America), Dublin (Europe), and Egypt (Africa), he was well on his way. For Charles, running marathons was also a way to spit in the face of the disease. "I gave up my fear of dying a long time ago," he said.

The next night was our orientation dinner, held in the ballroom of the hotel. At the cocktail hour preceding the dinner, I saw my other travel mates for the first time. They were loud and boisterous, shy and withdrawn; they were young and old, of all shapes and sizes. Some seemed to have come alone, others in groups. I met some of the "star" runners I'd heard about from the Marathon Tours people, including Nita Kay LeMay, the legally blind runner from outside Chicago, and William Tan from Singapore, the first wheelchair participant in this race. I met Dennis Martin, a fellow New Yorker. A broad-shouldered, low-key fellow who had the look of a very contented man, he was also not a guy you'd want to pick a fight with. A retired New York City Police Department officer, Dennis had spent years as part of Mayor Ed Koch's bodyguard detail. There was lean, white-haired

Ron Bucy, a sixty-year-old from West Virginia who had run 121 marathons since 1976. Ron, who was about to join the Seven Continents Club, was already a member of the 50 States Marathon Club, a group of runners who have completed a marathon in every state. (Ron had already outdistanced that pack, too; he was thirty-three states into his second time around the country!) On the other end of the spectrum were fifty-five-year-old David Ross and his eighteen-year-old son James Ross from Redmond, Washington. They had decided to run their first marathon together—in Antarctica. Had anyone suggested to them that Antarctica might not be the best place to run one's first marathon? David nodded. "Everyone! And most of them didn't put it so delicately. They told us we were flat-out crazy." James, with youthful bravado, didn't seemed fazed by the prospect of running twenty-six miles for the first time in his life in an environment barely suited for trudging one hundred yards. "It's cool," he said. "I know I can always walk if I have to." (The young man was perhaps channeling the spirit of another James Ross, the explorer who first surveyed the coast of the Antarctic mainland.)

There was a lot of boring talk about marathons completed, times, training mileage, and trail shoes. We also shared stories about the reactions we got from people at home when they heard where we were going. A runner from Michigan told me that when she told a local store clerk she was going to Antarctica, he didn't flinch. "That's nice," he said earnestly. "You got relatives down there?"

Gilligan invited me to join him at his table. I took a seat and found myself across from a handsome, dark-complexioned fellow. "John," Gilligan said, by way of introduction. "Gustavo. Our main man in Antarctica." Gustavo smiled. "Call me Gus," he said, in fluent English. Gustavo Papazian was a Buenos Aires native and

a trained biologist who had wintered at his country's Esperanza
base. Wintering over in Antarctica—staying from around April to
November, is a real badge of honor. Few do it. "What was it like?"
I asked. Gus grinned, revealing a mouth full of bright, white
teeth. "Cold," he replied. He was being modest. It turned out that
Gus's job had been studying penguins in the water, so he was also
a diver. In 1997 he went to work for Marine Expeditions, the outfit that originally helped Marathon Tours to set up the Antarctica
Marathon. He impressed Gilligan right away. Gus was a native
Spanish speaker, which was helpful to have on King George
Island, with its Chilean and Uruguayan bases; he was used to the
conditions of Antarctica; and, most important, he was a reliable
and good-natured guy. Thom was so impressed with his performance in the 1997 marathon that in subsequent editions he had
it written into his own contract that any expedition outfit handling the Antarctica Marathon had to hire Gus. He was Thom's
go-to guy for the race. I liked him immediately as well. Gus was
modest about his experience, despite spending a total of ten years
in Antarctica on various projects, a record probably matched by
very few. "Ten years!" I said. "That's incredible!" He blushed,
shrugged, and changed the topic, asking me about my running.
He wasn't a runner, he said, but he loved bicycling. I asked him
about the Tour de France, and his eyes lit up. We talked for an
hour about the next year's race, about some of the up-and-coming
young riders, and about whether Lance Armstrong would win
again (Gustavo thought he would, and he was right; he also predicted that another major drug scandal would hit the tour in the
next few years—and he was right about that, too). Here I was supposed to be interviewing runners about to run in Antarctica, and
instead I was talking about the Tour de France with an Argentine

bicycling fan. No matter. It was a pleasure to be in Gus's company. From that point on, every time I saw him—usually bustling around the ship on some task or another—he would stop and give me a big smile and a thumbs-up. I was glad I met Gus that night.

After dinner Gilligan got up onstage and addressed the audience. He started by reminding us again how desolate and remote it was where we were going. "The marathon starts at Bellingshausen, the Russian base on King George Island," he said. "You know, in Russia when kids are bad, they threaten to send them to Siberia. In Siberia when kids are bad, they threaten to send them to Bellingshausen." Thom went on to explain that the people stationed in Bellingshausen get so lonely that it's a big deal when the marathoners show up. Because the station crew helps out with the organization of the race, providing volunteers and allowing the runners to use some of their facilities, "we like to give something back to them. I'm asking everybody to please contribute a gift, candy bars, canned food, CDs, whatever . . . no hard liquor, please . . . that we can give them when we arrive."

Having told us about the lonely Russians, Gilligan told us a little about ourselves and the expedition that would begin shortly: There were 227 people—runners, staff, and crew—involved in the 2005 Antarctica Marathon. We would sail on two ships, built in Finland in 1987 and sold to the Russians, allegedly for scientific research but more likely for spying on U.S. submarines. They were specifically designed for the Antarctic and built to withstand eighty-mile-per-hour winds and sixty-foot-high seas.

Murmurs in the crowd.

He went on to discuss our motivations. "We've found that there are three reasons people go to Antarctica for the marathon," he said.

"Reason one . . . they're nuts!" called out a wiseacre.

Gilligan smiled and continued. "The first is adventure," he said. "People who are successful in their professional lives but were unfulfilled. Second, people who want to be an inspiration for family and friends. Third, people who raise funds for different charities." I was trying to figure out where I fit into this typology—how about people who decided to go to Antarctica instead of Las Vegas for their fiftieth birthday?—when Gilligan announced the single largest fundraiser in our group, Joe Hale, from Cincinnati, Ohio, who had raised $120,000 for the March of Dimes.

He ended his presentation by giving us our itinerary. One more day in Buenos Aires, and then on Tuesday, February 22, we would board a 5:30 A.M. flight for Ushuaia. "You need to make sure your bags are packed and in the main lobby by 3 A.M.," Gilligan said. Silence—jaws dropped around me. "Guess that means we'll just have to stay up all night," said the Gen X goofball with the tattoos at the next table. Not me. As the dinner broke out and groups of runners began to hail taxis to go enjoy the famous Buenos Aires nightlife, I went up to my room, took out from my bag the bottle of champagne that the steward on the plane from New York had given me, and brought it back down to Thom. "For the crew at Bellingshausen, with my compliments," I said. "They'll appreciate that," he said, admiring the label.

The next morning I got up for a run. I went down to the river, Rio de la Plata, and ran up and back along the plaza, at one point passing a ragged line of gray-sweatshirted police recruits, out for their morning exercise. I passed by the bigger guys in the back, who were sweating and panting. Passed the middle-level guys, who looked surprised to see a middle-aged gringo near them. Got up to the guys near the front. They looked at me; I looked at them. They picked up the pace; I picked up the pace. They picked it up even more. They were faster. I turned off and jogged back to the hotel. That was my speed work for the week—and probably my last run before the marathon, five days away.

After breakfast, I lifted weights in the hotel gym for an hour and got a massage. I wanted to tire myself out so that I could get to sleep really early that night, in time for the 2:30 A.M. wake-up call. We were on our way to the end of the Americas.

6

ENGLISH LESSONS, RUSSIAN RULES

Groggy and yawning, the group of marathoners trudged through the nearly empty airport. It was three thirty in the morning of February 22. I fell into step with a lanky, gray-haired man with a dignified, erect bearing. I nodded a greeting; he responded with a cheerful "Hulloo." English accent. Perfect! Who better to explore Antarctica with than a Brit?

While Antarctica may not "belong" to any one country, its early history is as British as biscuits and tea. It was an Englishman, after all, who first got near the place, the legendary Captain James Cook. Captain James Ross, who first surveyed the Antarctic coast, was also an Englishman. An Anglo-Irishman, Ernest Shackleton, came to define the courage needed to explore and survive the continent, and an Englishman, Captain Robert Falcon

Scott, was killed by it and became, as British writer Sara Wheeler puts it in her book *Terra Incognita*, "the central Antarctic myth . . . a man inextricably woven into the fabric of the national culture."

Francis Staples, the man I struck up a friendship with that morning, seemed part of that culture, too, an almost stereotypical part of it. His accent was upper class, the vowels as lush and rounded as a plump breakfast scone. He was a gangly beanpole of a fellow, with wispy gray hair, a mustache, and a to-the-manor-born bearing. I could well imagine him in a bowler and pin-striped suit, on his way to his job at Lloyd's of London, where he had worked as a broker until the previous month. When he turned sixty-five, he traded in that bowler and briefcase for a pair of running shoes and a duffel bag. Antarctica, he said, was "a retirement gift to myself." I tried to place Francis on the time line of recent British history and realized with a start that he was the same age as Ringo Starr. Yet he seemed a member of a very different generation than the ex-Beatle drummer, more out of the intrepid Scott and Shackleton era: a very proper, well-respected-man-about-town Brit who could also, on a whim, pick up and head off to the end of the Earth—which is exactly where he was now headed.

The job at Lloyd's had been a sedentary one, Francis said. Probably a lot of sitting at a desk, or on overstuffed easy chairs with clients at exclusive London clubs. So in his late forties Francis had taken up jogging. "The usual story," he said. "I started at lunchtime, and at first couldn't finish a mile. One thing led to another, and now here I am running a marathon in Antarctica. And if you had told me this is where I would end up, I would have said you were crazy." Francis's roommates on the ship would later tell me they did, in fact, think he was crazy. "Every morning he repacks all his clothes," one of them told me, as if this were some sure sign of clinical schizophrenia. To me it just confirmed Francis's delightful Englishness: he spoke with a slight stutter and did seem a bit eccentric, but he was sharp-witted and up for anything. On this trip he had plenty of company.

After three hours we winged out of the clouds to find ourselves over mountains. This was Tierra del Fuego, and below us was the Martial range, part of a chain that extended south from the Andes, under the Southern Ocean, and then reemerged, hundreds of miles south, as the imposing Transantarctic Mountains. As if foretelling their ultimate destination, the mountains grew white caps the farther south we went, and then, as the plane began its descent, they seemed to join in becoming one jaw of white and ice. Clutched in its center, and facing a wide, blue channel of water, was a patchwork of streets and the roofs of small buildings.

We had arrived in Ushuaia, the so-called Gateway to Antarctica.

There was a slight change in the weather when we disembarked in the little airport. Suddenly it was winter. The flip-flops, shorts, and tank tops of Buenos Aires were gone; now we were surrounded by fleece vests, hiking boots, and expedition hats. Ushuaia, nestled in a glacier at the very tip of the continent, is the southernmost city in the Americas. In recent years it has also become a popular tourist destination for outdoor activities, giving the sense that you have landed in a sort of Third World version of Aspen, Colorado. Americans and Europeans stride the dusty streets with expensive North Face backpacks and GPS watches, looking for sushi bars. On the bus ride into town, a guide told us a little about the city. Ushuaia, located two thousand miles south of Buenos Aires, is a tiny community by comparison, with a population of forty-five thousand. Down here,

borders blend; Argentina's Tierra del Fuego and Chile's Patagonia are merely two different names for what is essentially the same
archipelago—Argentina has the Atlantic coast, Chile, the Pacific.
Even Ushuaia has its opposite number in Chile's Punta Arenas,
a city on the northwest side of the archipelago that serves Antarctica by air. The 150-mile-long Beagle Channel, named after
Charles Darwin's ship, which sailed through here in the 1830s,
is also a shared border—and not always happily. In 1978 the two
countries almost went to war over three islands in the Channel.
Pope John Paul II sent an envoy to mediate. A treaty was signed
in 1984 that settled the dispute and pledged "peace and friendship" between the two nations.

Once the site of a penal colony, Ushuaia today has a different role, one not unlike that of the Midwest American towns in
the 1800s that served as the beginning point for the great wagon
train journeys into the unknown. The stakes for those pioneers
who went rolling out of places like Independence, Missouri, on
the Oregon Trail, were no doubt higher and the dangers greater.
Yet, one got a similar sense here in Ushuaia that this was a frontier town: the Antarctic frontier. All you had to do was walk along
the waterfront where the expedition ships docked to feel you were
on the edge of something big. From mid-November to mid-
March, these ships sailed back and forth from the harbor at
Ushuaia to the Antarctic Peninsula and the South Shetland
Islands.

According to the International Association of Antarctica Tour
Operators, thirty-five ships carried a total of 27,950 passengers
to the Antarctic, mostly from Ushuaia, in the 2004–2005 summer season. Of those, probably about fifteen vessels did most of
the heavy lifting, making at least eight to ten round-trips during

the four-month austral summer. These workhorses, originally
designed for science or spying, aren't luxury cruise liners. You're
never going to see them cruising into Aruba with a bunch of
American tourists crowding around the dessert table. For dealing with the extreme conditions of the Antarctic, however, these
old cold war relics are perfect, all built with shallow drafts and
reinforced hulls strong enough to plow through broken ice. The
names of these Antarctic expedition ships sound like something
out of a Soviet-era version of the board game Clue: *Professor
Molchanov, Aleksey Maryshev, Kapitan Khlebnikov, Grigoriy
Mikheev*. These marvelously rich Russian names seemed imbued
with a power all their own, as if their mere utterance could shat-
ter ice. ("*Kapitan Khlebnikov!*" Crraccckkk.) The dominance of
these ships, many of them built in the 1980s, in the Antarctic
tourist trade of the early twenty-first century, reminded us that
while the Soviet Union may not have been capable of producing
a viable economic system, it sure knew how to get around in
really cold places. Or as the ultra-right-wing, let's-nuke-Moscow
father of one of my best friends in high school used to say, with
grudging admiration, "The bastards are good in the snow." It's
true: the Brits may have led the way in the nineteenth and the
early twentieth century, but in the postwar and postcommunist
era, Russia ruled. "The Russians are the best in polar travel," one
veteran Antarctic hand told me. "No question about it."

The irony is that these mighty ships, built to help protect the
motherland from the imperialists, are now at the mercy of the
imperialists' free market. While they are still owned by the Russian government, the *Kapitan* and his buddies would probably be
rotting on the dock in Kaliningrad if it weren't for all the American, European, and Asian capitalists with the desire and cash to

visit Antarctica. Typically the ships—complete with Russian captain and crews—are leased or sold to tour operators, who gussy
them up with relatively comfortable passenger quarters and sell
trip packages to tourists. There are now so many cruises leaving
for Antarctica that, the guidebooks say, if you arrived in Ushuaia
to go kayaking, explore the abundant wildlife of Tierra del Fuego,
or climb its glaciers and you suddenly got a hankering to visit
Antarctica, you could probably find a last-minute deal. Or failing
that, one book says, "many Ushuaia travel agents will find alternative arrangements." I'm not sure you'd want to go to Antarctica using "alternative arrangements," but just in case, the option
is there. (And if you do, I'd make sure a Russian was involved
somewhere along the line.)

As the bus pulled up near the center of town, our guide bade
us farewell with what I suppose has become a typical Antarctica
tourist fare-thee-well. "I hope you have a nice Drake Passage,"
he said earnestly.

That reminded me: time to put on my seasickness patch.

We had a couple of hours to kill before we would board our
ship. Most of my fellow runners had invaded the souvenir shops.
I saw them walking about, holding giant, stuffed penguins and
sporting USHUAIA: FIN DEL MUNDO T-shirts. The "end of the
world," indeed. Ushuaia's unofficial slogan also happened to be
the name of its own marathon. That race was being held a week
after ours. So many of those aspiring Seven Continents runners
figured that while they were in Argentina, they might as well
check South America off the list as well. To satisfy them, Gilligan had arranged it so we could arrive back in Ushuaia from
Antarctica just in time to run Fin Del Mundo. Almost half of
our group—106 runners—had opted to do both races, mean-

ing that these nuts would run two marathons in the course of one week.

Not me. I would be happy to get through the one in Antarctica. First I had to get there, without leaving several of my lunches and dinners in the Drake Passage. I walked into a bistro, locked myself in the men's room, and fumbled around with the patch. I felt vaguely guilty in there, like a junkie shooting himself up while decent people sipped lattes and nibbled on croissants outside. I emerged with the patch placed securely behind my left ear. As I walked down the streets, I noticed it was a fairly common item, as if the entire city had suffered a mass outbreak of hearing problems.

Francis and I had agreed to meet for lunch. We were joined by two other English friends I had made, Ingrid Hall, a cute-as-a-button, tough-as-nails major in the British army, and her friend Amanda Payne, a glamorous, blond physician from London. We talked about our respective cultures, our upcoming adventure, running, and Antarctica over pizza at a picturesque little Italian restaurant just off Ushuaia's main street. I asked them if they knew about the story of Scott and his ill-fated expedition to the South Pole. They laughed. "Everyone in England knows about Scott," Francis said. The captain's famous "Message to the Public," written before he and two companions perished in their tent and found on his body by a rescue party months later, was required reading and memorized by several generations of English schoolchildren. In the foreword to her book on Scott, *A First Rate Tragedy*, author Diana Preston says that her curiosity about the man and his Antarctic expeditions was first piqued at the South Hampstead High School for Girls, where Scott's "Message to the Public" was prominently displayed, framed in oak, in the school's hallway. This oft-quoted portion of the "Message" reads:

> Had we lived, I should have had a tale to tell of the hardi-hood, endurance and courage of my companions which would have stirred the heart of every Englishman. These rough notes and our dead bodies must tell the tale. . . .

Ingrid, in her thirties, knew who Scott was, too, but her favorite character from that drama was Lawrence "Titus" Oates, the British army officer who was part of Scott's five-man team that reached the South Pole only to find out they'd been beaten by Amundsen and his party. Oates suffered frostbite on his feet during the long, doomed march back, and in a blizzard, near the end, he gallantly sacrificed his own life so that his three remaining comrades wouldn't have to expend further energy carrying him along. His famous last words, as he crawled out of their miserable tent into a howling blizzard: "I am just going outside and may be some time." I suppose a more learned observer of British society might have gleaned some significance in the way two different generations, personified by Francis and Ingrid, identified with two different characters in that great polar tragedy: Scott, the man of many words, Oates, the man of very few.

With my stomach knotting up as we got closer to the boarding time, I went to a phone booth after lunch and made one last call to my wife. I tried to keep it light, telling her how I had fumbled around in the bathroom with the seasickness patch, carefully aiming it, and worried that I might slip and accidentally stick it on my cheek or temple, where it would have had to remain for two weeks. But my real feelings at that moment weren't about seasickness, but homesickness. Just four days away from family—we still had two weeks to go—and I was already homesick. We said good-bye, she far more cheerfully than I, and back out to the streets of Ushuaia I went.

One more errand to do before heading over to the docks. I'm not sure why I thought I would need more cash, since there was no place to spend it in Antarctica, but I decided to go to an ATM machine at a local bank. When I put my card up to the horizontal slot, it was sucked in as if a vacuum cleaner had gotten hold of it. I made my transaction, got my cash, and then waited for my card to reappear at the same slot, as they do in most American ATMs. Nothing. I poked around, hit various buttons. Still nothing. Now I started to panic, because I realized that in an hour I would be boarding a ship for ten days, giving up all contact with the outside world. At the very least, I imagined headaches and hassles with my bank—all of which would be in the back of my mind for the next two weeks. I went up to the customer service area and waited nervously in line, cursing card-sucking Third World technology under my breath. When it was my turn, I tried to explain in halting English what had happened. The woman behind the desk tried patiently to understand, but couldn't. "The machine ate my card," I said in a panicked voice. Her brow furrowed. I chastised myself for not speaking better Spanish or carrying a pocket dictionary. Just then, a man from the next line appeared, holding my card. Speaking in Spanish and gesturing back to the ATM machine, he was about to hand it over to another customer service rep. "That's mine!" I practically screamed. I grabbed the card out of his hand, and as the poor fellow, two customer service reps, and several others in line looked at me in shocked silence, I mumbled *"gracias"* and scurried out of the bank. At the moment

I was walking out the door, a woman was at the same cash machine, finishing up a transaction. I noticed that she reached down into the bottom tray to retrieve her cash, along with her card. That's where mine had been all along. This was the fault not of Argentine technology but an American's stupidity. *What an idiot you are*, I thought to myself. *You're going to Antarctica? You can't even get cash out of an ATM.*

It was time to get out of this funk and into a new frame of mind. A trip to Antarctica is a great remedy for this, provided you're not planning to spend the dark winter there, which, as numerous studies and several gory murders on remote scientific stations have proven, can drive you insane. Many compare the whiteness of the place to the blank page on a new chapter in one's life. Despite what Thom had said in his speech in Buenos Aires, this slate cleaning seemed to be the motivating factor for many of my fellow runners. Among our group there were a high number of people recently divorced, recently retired, recently recovered, or maybe, like me, recently feeling their mortality and age.

The sign on the sea wall at Ushuaia seemed to sum up what we all wanted out of it: THE END OF THE WORLD, THE BEGINNING OF EVERYTHING. Or at least, we hoped, something.

At about three thirty that afternoon, the gates opened and a hundred runners clattered up the ramp of the *Akademik Sergey Vavilov*, which gleamed in the afternoon sun, pearly white, its hull festooned with a fascinating array of mysterious-looking appendages—antennae, cranes, poles. This sturdy Russian ship would be our home for the next ten days. It would also mark our beginning as a little floating community. Half of the runners who would run the Antarctica Marathon were at a hotel in Ushuaia. They would be boarding their ship, the *Vavilov*'s twin, *Akademik*

Ioffe, the next morning. We would see no more of them until race day.

On board the *Vavilov* we were greeted with a barrage of instructions: "Hand in your passport, please. Leave your bags there. Here's your room assignment." It was all so well organized, especially considering the international cast of characters involved. Like the governance of the continent itself, the Antarctica Marathon was a joint venture among various nations. There was the U.S.-based Marathon Tours, of course, which included Thom Gilligan and a small team of road race professionals, including the stalwart Gustavo I had met in Buenos Aires, who would help with timing and course management during the marathon. There was the Russian crew; and then there was Peregrine Adventures, the Vancouver-based expedition tour group. The Peregrine staff on our trip, mostly Australians and Canadians, handled all our excursions once we got to Antarctica and were also responsible for keeping us informed and entertained on the way down. This they would do through lectures, after-dinner talks, the posting of a daily ship's log to help us keep track of our progress, announcements over the ship's PA system, and an almost incessant stream of invitations to the observation deck for cocktails, meals in the dining room, or coffee, tea, and snacks on the bridge. Anyone who accepted even half of the epicurean hospitality offered by this Peregrine bunch would have actually gained weight on the marathon trip.

I made my way through a bewildering array of ladders and doors, opened my door, and found myself in a ten-foot-long-by-six-foot-wide cabin with bunk beds, a desk and chair, two closets, a sink with a medicine cabinet, and a porthole. It looked, I supposed, like a dorm room at Kaliningrad State Technical University: spartan and cramped but livable. A second later I learned that it was going to be even cozier when my roommate arrived. He was William Tan, the wheelchair competitor from Singapore. The gentleman that he is, William immediately began apologizing. "I'm sorry," he said. "I told them it might be difficult for you to share one of these small rooms with me in my chair. But Thom thought it would be a good way for you to interview me." He had a point. I had been assigned by the *Boston Globe* to write a profile of William, and I'd certainly get to know him now. As it turned out, bunking with William would, for me, prove to be one of the great blessings of Antarctica—not only because living with a disabled person gave me new perspective, but also because he is one of the most inspirational and able people I've ever met.

William was born in 1957. His parents, poor and uneducated, had moved to Singapore from mainland China shortly after his birth. They didn't know that a vaccine for polio had been recently discovered, and when William contracted the disease at age two, it was too late. He lost the use of his legs, and over the course of his childhood he was encouraged to develop his mind instead. He became an excellent student, but he yearned for a more active life. There were no physical education classes for children with disabilities in those days. "I was confined to the classroom, staring out the window watching other children play," William recalled sadly, when we had a heart-to-heart. He started playing Ping-Pong in the school's rec room, sometimes by himself, just volleying off the wall. Then he heard about a police officer who had been paralyzed in the line of duty and had subsequently started a disabled sports program in another part of Singapore. "At age seventeen, I bravely took a taxi to a stadium looking for this man," William said. He found him and also learned that the officer was using not an old, hospital-style wheelchair but rather a new kind of sleek, lightweight chair, a chair designed to go fast and maneuver deftly. "He let me have a go on his race wheelchair around the track." The feeling of pushing, moving, of going fast under his own propulsion was something new to him. "It was exhilarating," he said. "I had never had the sense of speed."

William was soon involved in the burgeoning sport of wheelchair athletics, training hours a day on his chair. "It was an instant passion. It must have been all that confined energy." By the time I met him, he had become a topflight competitive wheelchair marathoner—one of many who competed at races like the Boston, Los Angeles, and New York City marathons. A competitive wheelchair division, once a curiosity, was now a fixture at most major marathons. The "chairs," as they call themselves, had earned the right to race, win prize money, and be treated like any other athlete. A few even make a living from it.

While he enjoyed racing, William had other professional goals, one of which seemed to be a desire to earn every advanced degree and honor known to humankind. He had gotten pretty far down the list: university scholarship, Ph.D. in neuroscience, research fellowship at the Mayo Clinic, Fulbright scholarship to the Harvard School of Public Health, and, most recently, completion of medical school in Australia. He was William Tan, Ph.D., M.D., MPH, and CG—certified genius.

William was also fundraising for children's cancer research. He had a particular child in mind: Jessica Doktor, a six-year-old girl from Ipswich, Massachusetts. While William was at Harvard on his Fulbright, he had met Jessica and her parents at Boston's Children's Hospital. The two became close friends. William, who knew what it was like to be a child with a serious illness, said he was inspired by Jessica's fight. A total of six times, he would dedicate his Boston Marathon to Jessica; and several times he crossed the finish line with the little girl in his lap. "She's a little hero to me," he said of Jessica.

When he called Marathon Tours in late 2004 asking to participate in the Antarctica Marathon as part of his efforts to raise money to fight children's cancer and to be the first wheelchair athlete to complete a marathon on all seven continents, Gilligan hesitated. He tried to visualize navigating a wheelchair across cold, glacial streams, loose rocks, and ice for 26.2 miles. "I thought, *No way*," Gilligan said. Still, he was intrigued enough to do a web search on Tan and, like everyone else, was enormously impressed by what he found. In a follow-up conversation, Tan told him he hoped to run the marathon in Antarctica as part of an attempt at completing seven marathons in seven continents in seventy days, culminating with Boston on April 18. Each race would be a fundraiser for charities, including Children's Hospital, where Jessica was treated and where Gilligan's wife, Sharon, is a nurse. That clinched it for Thom. "I called him and said, 'William, let's take a shot at Antarctica and see what happens."

As William finished telling me his life story, we were interrupted by the crackle of a tiny loudspeaker in our room. Over it came a female voice with an Australian accent, as smooth and rich as honey. "Hell-ooo," it said, sounding as if instead of being piped in over a second-rate 1980s public address system, each word was being poured slowly and deliciously out of a jar. "Welcome aboard. This is Annie; I'm the hostess on the ship. We hope you're getting settled in, and we're looking forward to sailing with you on your marathon adventure. First, we have the mandatory lifeboat drill. So please assemble in five minutes on the main deck."

William and I decided that we would follow that voice anywhere. So with me giving his chair a little help over and around various obstacles on board, we made our way out onto the deck. There a wiry, ruggedly handsome fellow named Jack gave us an entertaining demonstration on what we should do if there was an emergency at sea—entertaining because, as Jack made clear, while the odds of an emergency at sea were slim, if there was one in Antarctica, and we had to actually crowd into these stifling lifeboats, we were pretty much screwed. The good news was that a fast solution was at hand: two minutes in the Antarctic waters, Jack told us, and we'd freeze to death. He grinned. "Well, that's the drill; congratulations, you've passed. Now would you join us for a cocktail on the observation desk?" Soon, we were sipping drinks on the observation deck, which doubled as a bar. At one point I looked out and noticed that Ushuaia was slipping into the distance. The sun was setting, and the Beagle Channel lay ahead. A few lights sparkled on the land in the distance—the last few miles of America, as we approached the end of the continent. Later that night, as we slept, the *Vavilov* left the pilot ship behind, slipped out of the channel and into the Drake Passage, to begin our two-day, 750-mile journey south to the Antarctic Peninsula.

I awoke to a thumping outside. Startled, I poked my head out from my top bunk and thought I saw a gray-haired face flash, like a chimera, outside our porthole. Was I dreaming? Was this the ghost of some long-departed whaler or Russian *refusenik*? I looked down at William. He was still sleeping. I lay back, trying to get used to the gentle rocking sensation I felt around me, and then . . . there was the face again. This time I clambered out of bed, dropped onto the floor as quietly as I could, slipped on sweat clothes, and stepped outside on the deck—just in time to see a jogger disappear behind a gangway. Considering the *Vavilov* is 387 feet long, he was going to have to do a lot of laps, I thought, to cover even a few miles. The mystery solved, I was about to turn around and head back to my bunk, when I looked up.

We were surrounded entirely by water.

This was the first time I'd ever been in the middle of the ocean with no land in sight. The sight of nothing but limitless blue sky and green, white-capped sea took my breath away. I stepped back inside, popped my head into the bunk, where my roommate was just stirring. "William," I said, softly. "I am just going outside, and may be some time."

The Drake Lake Effect

7

The ship rising and settling gracefully on the white-capped waves, the rhythmic inhalations of the sea around us, the boundless sky and empty horizons: I stood at the head of the ship, taking it all in.

If a body of water has a personality, the Drake Passage is manic-depressive, prone to fits of rage, alternating with periods of docile languor. Mariners have their own way of describing the water's contrasting moods. "Nasty, vile, cruel, unmerciful, Devil's dance floor and the meanest piece of sea on the face of the planet" was the descriptive epithet of one mariner. Andrew Prossin, the leader of the Peregrine group on the *Vavilov*, was more succinct in his assessment of the five-hundred-mile passage. "It's either the Drake Lake or the Drake Shake," he said. Despite his boyish looks, Prossin, a native of Nova Scotia, had led over one hundred expeditions to Antarctica. It was he who gave us daily briefings at breakfast and dinner, updating us on our progress as we made our way across. "We've got the Lake so far," he said that morning. "Let's hope it stays that way."

Scientists believe the Passage was formed thirty to fifty million years ago when the continents of South America and Antarctica split apart. The opening that was created provided a gateway between the Pacific and Atlantic oceans, a sort of natural "fast lane" for water to go roaring around the globe, unimpeded at this latitude. Now known as the Atlantic Circumpolar Current, this powerful surge transports an incredible 426 million cubic feet of water through the relatively narrow Drake Passage every second. In addition, the prevailing winds at this latitude—the so-called westerlies—are persistent and strong, helping to whip up waves and swells. Then there's the presence, at about sixty degrees south, of the Antarctic Convergence, the point where the Atlantic and Pacific meet the Southern Ocean, which surrounds Antarctica. (Many believe the Convergence marks the continent's true border.) All of these factors—powerful current, persistent winds, cooler and warmer waters colliding—combine to make the Drake Passage one of the most turbulent and unpredictable bodies of water in the world. Waves of over thirty feet in height are not uncommon. Neither, apparently, are the rather gentle swells that continued to roll along during our first day at sea. After breakfast, I stared out at these still-calm waters for another hour before it was time to attend the first of several mandatory lectures.

Going to Antarctica is considered a privilege by its stewards, and they want you to appreciate that. We tourists were expected to learn something about the place we were visiting in the hopes that we would go home with a greater understanding of its fragility and value. One thing we learned is that Antarctica is one of the few places where international cooperation has actually worked. Since 1961, when the Antarctic Treaty was put into effect, the continent has been jointly administered by sixteen nations but "owned" by none. The treaty's main purpose is to ensure "in the interests of all mankind that Antarctica shall continue forever to be used exclusively for peaceful purposes and shall not become the scene or object of international discord." Both the United States and the USSR were among the original signatories, which, when you consider the discord between them at that point—the Bay of Pigs invasion, the Cuban Missile Crisis—is rather extraordinary. The leaders of these two armed-to-the-teeth nuclear superpowers, constantly seeking an edge over the other, were able to somehow look toward the bottom of the globe and instead of seeing a strategic advantage, instead of seeing it as a good site for another missile base, decided that they ought to just . . . leave it alone. To keep Antarctica, as the treaty stipulates, "a natural reserve dedicated to peace and science."

That's pretty much how it's been ever since, although some see trouble on the horizon. While the treaty remains in force indefinitely, pressure is already building from some of the smaller nations involved, notably Argentina and Chile, both of which have long viewed parts of Antarctica as sort of southerly extensions of Patagonia and Tierra del Fuego. Supposedly some in those countries want to amend the treaty and begin some limited form of economic development, at least on the Antarctic Peninsula. Others worry that the increasing energy needs of the developed world will inevitably result in oil and natural gas exploitation. No one doubts that the reserves there are enormous. Will an oil-hungry world be able to resist the temptation?

▲ ▲ ▲

For the time being, however, the treaty holds. Since there are no people there, the prime beneficiaries are the birds and sea mammals, especially those cuddly cute penguins that seem to define the continent and have become such a part of popular culture. Don't get me wrong: I love the whales, the penguins, the seals, and all the rest—and I do believe they should be left in peace. It's just that I'm not so enthralled with them that I want to learn about their personal lives. I don't particularly feel as if I need to learn which kind of seal eats which kind of fish, how they mate, what they feed their young, and all sorts of other intimate secrets. So I found myself drifting off as an animated naturalist named Ziggy—so-called because he was very fond of David Bowie music—led us through our second lecture of the day, about the Antarctic wildlife we were going to encounter. As he talked and ran through his PowerPoint presentation, many of my fellow runners were sitting on the edge of their seats in the *Vavilov's* little semicircular lecture hall, several almost in tears when they heard about the various horrible ways that some of these big Antarctic birds will kill little penguin chicks, particularly the pelican, which, as Ziggy explained in gory detail, scoops up a little baby, keeping it alive in its mouth for a few horrifying moments before regurgitating the bewildered little bird at a spot safe enough for the pelican to then peck it to pieces and eat it.

Maybe that's why I'm happy simply knowing wildlife is out there without getting too many of the details of how they pass their days and satisfy their daily nutritional requirements.

The next topic was whales. We would surely see some once we entered Antarctic waters, Ziggy promised, which provoked an excited murmuring in our group. He then played us a recording of the sounds whales use to communicate with one another. Everybody leaned in to hear an odd array of pops, hisses and whistles, and electronic-sounding warbles. Ziggy explained that this was the mating call or the danger signal of this or that whale, and as he did, I found myself reeling with an odd sense of déjà vu. I had heard these noises somewhere before. Where? How?

Suddenly my mind was transported through time and space. I was in an old brownstone on Commonwealth Avenue in the Back Bay section of Boston, which in those days, before rampant condo conversion, served as a dormitory for Emerson College. It was fall 1973, my freshman year at Emerson. While Thom Gilligan was probably running nearby with the Greater Boston Track Club, I was sitting around with three other long-haired guys in our dorm room, passing around a joint, and watching our friend Mike Sylvia, a fellow from New Bedford, Massachusetts, with bronze skin and shoulder-length hair, bouncing around the room playing an imaginary ensemble of instruments—drums, guitar, and synthesizer— while behind him a pair of giant JBL speakers blasted Edgar Winter's "Frankenstein," a big hit that year and still a staple on classic rock radio. There's this bit at the end of the instrumental song when Winter does a sort of synth breakdown, where it just hums like a giant engine that's running out of gas, descending from a very high to very low pitch, going *wahwahwahwahwahwuh, wuh,wuh,wuh,wuh, bub . . . bub . . . bub . . . bub . . . bub.* Then the music swirls around in an audio cloud, the synthesizer emitting a cacophony of odd electronic hisses, pops, and burps.

That's it, I thought! Whale mating sounds! That's where I'd heard them! What a wild time and a great song that was. . . . "Excuse me," said a woman, looking at me strangely. She was wearing a ski cap with an embroidered penguin on it. "Would you mind not banging your fist on my chair?" I looked around to make sure no one else had noticed. "Uhhh . . . sorry," I said, and then skulked out of the room, since Ziggy had moved on to crabeater seals.

After sitting in talks all morning about whales, penguins, and the Antarctic treaty, I needed to get back out on the deck, take in some fresh air, and stare out into the quiet abyss. Again, I made my way up to the observation deck, climbed down and through the maze of ladders and hatchways, out onto the foredeck and into my little dreaming post at the prow of the ship. We were motoring along at fourteen knots per hour, a brisk pace in the Passage, making good time thanks to the calm seas. Even the Russian crew, who maintained an icy distance from the passengers, seemed to sense it. As I tromped around the deck, I caught two of the crewmen laughing, seemingly in good spirits. (They stopped laughing as soon as I walked by.)

Not everybody was at the lecture or enjoying the seas. I noticed that several people were missing, including my buddy Dan, a writer for a major national sports magazine who was on assignment to write about William Tan and his attempt to become the first person to complete the Antarctica Marathon in a wheelchair. A midwesterner with a dry, sardonic wit, Dan was having major seasickness problems, even in the Drake Lake. I didn't see him until late in the day, emerging from the bathroom, a place that I gathered he had seen much of during the course of the day. He looked pale, miserable. "This sucks," he said.

This is fabulous, I thought to myself. I felt bad for Dan, but I couldn't help it if I wasn't seasick—the seas were calm, and I just couldn't get enough of it. Meanwhile, just to be sure, I followed old Jules Winkler's advice and took seconds at every meal. That the food was delicious and plentiful didn't hurt.

I was feeling so good and had so much to see—which, in retrospect, was really nothing more than empty sea and sky and an occasional albatross—that I couldn't sit still. Through the afternoon I continued walking around the deck like a windup doll, and each time I bumped into another runner I hadn't met—somebody else popping up for air, to take photos, or to ascertain that he or she wasn't dreaming, that after all the preparations and training, all the forms and flights, we were at last on our way to Antarctica. One of them was Dr. Rohit Vasa, who was also enjoying the Drake Lake. Vasa, a neonatologist from Chicago, had already run forty-six marathons. He was another of the many competitors, like William Tan, who had come here to achieve some kind of marathon first: "I hope to be the first person of Indian descent to run the marathon in Antarctica . . . and to do seven continents," he said proudly. But he was driven by more than the prospect of bragging rights among his friends and family. Doing this, doing anything to challenge himself, seemed to be part of his nature, a personality trait he shared with many on this ship. "One can sit back and relax and say, 'this is good enough for me,'" Rohit said. "But everyone is capable of doing something more than they are already doing. I believe in testing that. When you do that, when you challenge yourself, life is more fulfilling."

For Vasa and many others, Antarctica represented the next test, the next challenge, but for another runner—one I met while browsing through the *Vavilov*'s amply stocked library—coming to Antarctica was a way of connecting with the past. Ellyn Brown came from the other side of the globe—Alaska. She was studying the huge wall map of Antarctica that hung on the library wall, when I walked in. We started talking. It turned out that Ellyn's father, J. Linsley Gressit, was a prominent entomologist. From 1959 to 1961, in the very flush of the Antarctic Treaty era, her father came here for several months on a National Science Foundation grant to study parasites (it's estimated today that there are about sixty-seven species of insects in Antarctica, most of them the kind of tiny parasite-like creatures Gressit was studying). Ellyn recalls what it was like when her dad would return after a season on the ice. "He'd come back with a big red beard," she said, with a chuckle. It must have been an exciting time for Gressit. The treaty was signed in 1959 and went into effect two years later, so he was doing in Antarctica just what the international community had agreed should be done there—science. He later published a book on the entomology of the continent, and Ellyn says there is even a landmark on the continent named after him: Gressit Glacier. Sadly, he died in a plane crash in 1982. Ellyn, who now teaches middle school science in Anchorage, always wanted to visit the far-off land her father loved. As a runner, this seemed the way to do it. "He would have been proud of me, I think," she said. "But I think he would have preferred it if I had come down here for science."

As opposed to running in circles around a glaciated island? She was probably right about that. Just eight years after the Antarctic Treaty was signed, the first Antarctic tourist ship, the *Lindblad Explorer*, was launched by Swedish explorer Lars-Eric Lindblad, sparking a debate that goes on today. There are those who feel that no tourism should be permitted here at all, that the continent should be left to the ice and the penguins and the moss and those studying them. A truce was eventually hammered out, and the tour operators were grudgingly allowed in, but only under clear stipulations. These were, essentially, that any tourists they would bring to Antarctica would not behave like tourists do in most other parts of the world. First and foremost, this meant having minimal environmental impact. There are pages of resolutions

and international laws that the operators must adhere to, man-
dating everything from waste disposal (basically, you bring back
what you produce; nothing is dumped or left in Antarctica) to contact with the wildlife (don't get too close, for their safety). There
are even regulations about where you can set foot and how (carry
in on your shoes a few of the wrong germs from New York City
or Buenos Aires, and you could infect an entire penguin rookery).
This, of course, was one reason it was so difficult for Gilligan to
get permission for the marathon back in the mid-1990s. Two
hundred runners: that's a lot of feet covering a lot of ground on
Antarctica.

Founded in 1991, the sixty-nine-member International Association of Antarctica Tour Operators is quick to pay homage to
the powerful science lobby while asserting its right to do what it
does. Acknowledging in their literature that scientific research
remains "the primary focus for human presence in Antarctica," the
tour operators go on to argue that "Antarctica belongs to the people of the world. The more people can see and experience it in
an environmentally responsible way, the better chance it will be
well managed for future generations."

Some are not quite sure whether science and tourism here can
ever be compatible. Others think that, provided that ship toilets
aren't being emptied into the Southern Ocean or hot dog stands
constructed on the shores of the Ross Sea, the tourist industry
brings to the continent a much-needed spirit that's lacking in the
cloistered bases in the interior of the continent. In *Life on the Ice:
No One Goes to Antarctica Alone*, a chronicle of his months in
Antarctica, writer Roff Smith expressed frustration with the attitude of the scientific community, many of whom seemed bereft
of any sense of wonder at or exhilaration over the amazing place

they were studying. Rather, most scientists Smith met there seemed insistent on demonstrating the clinical detachment that is such a tiresome feature of academia. In other words, these scientists acted as if Antarctica was merely a chillier annex of their university labs. By contrast, Smith writes, the tourists "come down here for the sheer joy of it . . . for the thrill of seeing so much wildlife and the romance of distance. What's more, unlike scientists, tourists pay their own way, don't intrude on the landscape by building bases, and make no pretense of control or ownership."

We got a sense of that excitement around midday, when an announcement crackled over the ship's PA system. "We've got a school of porpoises swimming along with us starboard." A stampede of passengers brandishing digital cameras and recorders flooded the decks. Fortunately I was tucked into my little nook in the prow and had a perfect view: there they were, three dolphins, slicing through the waves to a chorus of "oohs" and "aahs" from the passengers and the accompanying snaps, clicks, and whirs of their photographic equipment. According to the detailed wildlife sightings log kept by Ziggy during the trip, these were hourglass dolphins, about five feet long, stocky, with a large, curved dorsal fin. This is the only type of dolphin seen in Antarctic waters, and what little we know of them is based on a total of only twenty specimens—a reminder of how much about this continent and the creatures that live here remains a mystery.

Equally enthralling to me was the wandering albatross that followed in our wake for a while, circling the ship and then wheeling around and gliding back off into the horizon. Would this one portend the storms we had been told would suddenly turn the lake into the shake? They're out there, we knew; storms were constantly circling the continent. Some said it was just a matter of time before one of them hit the *Vavilov*. None ever did—and later I learned that an albatross was actually seen as a *good* omen (unless, of course, you killed it).

That evening I took one last walk around the deck before heading in. The sea was still calm, the horizon empty. Late the next day we were expected to spot land. As I popped back inside, I saw one of the Russian crew members emerge from a dark corridor. His eyes were bloodshot, and he had one hand on the bulkhead for support. He was clearly drunk and had apparently staggered out of his hiding place to get a good glimpse of Ingrid and her roommate, who were walking down the hallway from their cabin to the mess hall. He spun around when he heard me and scuttled away. I thought about reporting him but then I imagined myself mysteriously falling off the ship during one of my walks the next morning. Just then another member of the crew, who appeared to be a senior man, came stomping in from outside. He walked past me and down the dark corridor whence the drunken sailor had emerged. Seconds later I heard some sharp words in Russian and the sound of feet descending a hidden stairway.

Later, I shared this with a couple of new friends. "Watch, any minute now we'll hear an announcement, 'dolphins on the starboard side,'" joked Mark Ferguson. "Everyone will run over to that side of the ship, and meanwhile, while we're all looking for the dolphins, they'll assemble a firing squad on the other side, shoot the drunk guy, and dump him in the ocean." I had met Mark and his two colleagues, Bill Wrobel and Tim Rumford, through Ingrid at dinner. I liked them immediately, and when I found out they worked for a private space agency outside Washington, D.C., I started calling them "the Rocket Scientists." Which they were, although so self-deprecating and good-humored you would never imagine that these young men had the responsibility, not to mention the expertise, to launch multimillion-dollar satellites into outer space.

While we laughed about the drunken crewman, there was a part of me that felt sympathy for the remote, narrow-eyed men in whose gnarled hands were held our lives. The Russians seemed to get along with the Peregrine team, but one got the sense that, at least on this ship, they were under orders to stay away from the passengers and to make themselves as invisible as possible, as if seeing them would somehow spoil our fun. That had to rankle them. Here they were, sailing around the Antarctic for months at a time, separated from their families, doing hard physical labor in harsh conditions, and meanwhile they had to watch all of these spoiled Westerners prancing around their decks having a gay old time. Some of these crewmen perhaps had once been part of a proud Soviet navy, protecting the motherland from the imperialists. Now they had to do our bidding, just another part of the vast service contingent that must assemble whenever Americans arrive. It must have been a bitter pill for some to swallow, one that probably needed to be washed down with copious amounts of alcohol. I ran into that same fellow around the ship a few times during the course of the trip. He appeared sober and busy doing his work, and he never made eye contact with me.

When I got back to my cabin, I found William sitting at the desk reading my book on Scott and Amundsen. "Oh, hi," he said. "Hope you don't mind I'm reading this." Not at all, I assured him. "Thank you," he said. "It's fascinating." I noticed he was already halfway through. *Not only a genius*, I thought, *but a speed-reading genius to boot*. Feeling inadequate, I climbed up to my top berth.

In the middle of the night, I woke up to use the bathroom. Getting there was a little more difficult than I had imagined. First I slammed my head on the low ceiling. Then I bashed my foot against the bedpost as I tried to feel my way for the ladder. Finally, I missed a rung and came crashing down on the floor. Luckily William was a heavy sleeper and never rose. I picked myself up and, holding on from one railing to the next, lurched down the hallway to the bathroom, where I had to hold another railing with one hand as I relieved myself. Then I lurched back to our cabin. This became the pattern whenever I had to get up. Slam, bash, crash, lurch.

As I finally plopped myself back down in my bunk, I felt an odd sensation. It was the rocking of the ship on the waves, up and down, ever so gently. I felt like an infant, lying on the chest of its parent, rising and lowering as the parental chest expanded and contracted. Except here, it was the deep breath of something vast and unknowable—but reassuring nonetheless. To its deep, primordial rhythms, I fell peacefully asleep.

Rita Clark from Green Bay, Wisconsin, and friend in 1997. Needled for being a Cheesehead, she ended up earning kudos among her fellow travelers for becoming the premier Antarctic "butt skier."

PHOTO COURTESY OF RITA CLARK

Fred Lipsky, 1999. Tales of his trip to what he called "another planet" inspired the author to follow in Lipsky's muddy footsteps.

PHOTO COURTESY OF FRED LIPSKY

Ed Sylvester (*left*) and Thom Gilligan at the start of the 1995 Antarctica Marathon. MY NEXT HUSBAND WILL BE NORMAL read the sweatshirt that Sylvester's wife wore on race day— and as he prepared to run more than twenty-six miles on a course that had been hastily mapped out the previous day by Gilligan, he was probably thinking she was right.

PHOTO COURTESY OF ED SYLVESTER

All feet on deck, 2001. Stymied by the weather, the 2001 Antarctica Marathon earned its niche in running lore by being the first organized marathon to be held entirely on a ship. Photo by Marc Chalufour; reprinted with permission

The *Lyubov Orlova* in Neko Harbor, 2001. Named after a Russian movie star of the 1930s, the ship provided a bizarre but happy ending for the runners of the 2001 trip, who ran 26.2 miles around its decks. PHOTO BY MARC CHALUFOUR; REPRINTED WITH PERMISSION

Jules Winkler, 2001. The oldest runner on the 2001 marathon trip, Winkler, then seventy-one, ate his way to Antarctica—and as a result, he claims, never got seasick. PHOTO COURTESY OF JULES WINKLER

Darryn Zawitz in Ushuaia, 2005. From here, "the end of the world," we set sail for Antarctica and the 2005 marathon, a race that Zawitz, a thirty-five-year-old pilot from Pittsburgh, would win. PHOTO COURTESY OF DARRYN ZAWITZ

Sunset on the Drake Passage, 2005. This must be the Passage on Prozac; the notoriously schizophrenic waterway remained calm for the 2005 trip. PHOTO BY JOHN HANC

Loneliest grave on Earth, 2005. A simple cross for one of the thirty-five men, mostly Norwegian whalers, buried on Deception Island. PHOTO BY JOHN HANC

Ingrid Hall stashes her gear prior to the start of the 2005 Antarctica Marathon. This British army officer was unfazed by the ice, rocks, or "mood" that slowed most of the other runners. PHOTO COURTESY OF INGRID HALL

The author (*second from left*) in the Antarctica Marathon, 2005. My first time up the glacier and I'm looking pretty strong, right? Notice you won't find any photos here from the second time. PHOTO BY JIM BOKA; REPRINTED WITH PERMISSION

The Rocket Scientists launch into their postrace celebration, 2005. Mark Ferguson, Tim Rumford, and Bill Wrobel (*left to right*) enjoy stogies while proudly displaying their race numbers. PHOTO COURTESY OF MARK FERGUSON

The author with the Bicycle-Riding Grandmas. Thanks to the chutzpah of Shirl Kenney (*second from right*), she and her friends Joan Irwin (*left*) and Sharlene Anderson (*right*) set an unofficial record for riding a bike on all seven continents on the day of the 2005 Antarctica Marathon. PHOTO BY JOHN HANC

Amanda Payne, 2005. In some ways, wrote the British pediatrician in early 2008, "it seems like a lifetime ago." PHOTO COURTESY OF AMANDA PAYNE

The *Ioffe* and *Vavilov*, 2007. Stalwart veterans of the cold war, these former Russian sub trackers must now ferry imperialist running dogs to the bottom of the globe. PHOTO BY DAVID MCGONIGAL; COURTESY OF THOM GILLIGAN/MARATHON TOURS

Andvord Bay, Antarctica. The Last Continent just as we had always pictured it. PHOTO BY JOHN HANC

THE MADNESS OF KING GEORGE ISLAND

8

In the last years of his life, King George III descended into a strange, frightening world of delusion and madness.

The mysterious disease that had affected the English monarch earlier in his reign—a period that was later dramatized in a play and the award-winning 1994 film *The Madness of King George*—had returned with a vengeance. George, by then in his seventies, deaf, and blind, spent his days in Windsor Castle, a bearded, ghostlike figure. The world he once knew had moved on. The rebellion by his American colonies was almost thirty years in the past. Napoleon had been defeated. His own country was in the midst of an industrial revolution that had transformed the seemingly simpler, bucolic England that "Farmer George" so loved into an island of steam-powered factories and mills.

By late 1819 George had retreated into a world where, in the words of his biographer Christopher Hibbert, "the dead were alive, and the alive were dead." Though often docile, he was occasionally agitated and had to be placed in a straightjacket. At one point, Hibbert notes, he "talked for fifty-four hours with scarcely a moment's intermission." He was also subject to strange delusions and sometimes seemed to believe he possessed supernatural powers. One is tempted to wonder just how far these flights of fancy took the aged Hanoverian king—all the way to the bottom of the world, perhaps? Because at the very same time George was wandering the halls of Windsor, a prisoner of diminished senses and disease, a crew of his subjects were landing on the shore of a desolate, snow-peaked island, a new land that they would name after their sovereign.

The man who commanded that crew, the loyal subject of the mad, dying, but beloved king, was a twenty-nine-year-old sailor with the pedestrian name of William Smith. While he is largely forgotten in the history of Antarctic expedition, the black-haired, five-foot eight-inch Smith stands tall—not only for his discoveries but also for his tenacity and loyalty to his country. Smith grew up in Blyth, a community of laborers, blacksmiths, millers, and ship masters, a "vigorous industrial world," in the words of one scholar. Apprenticed to sea at about the age of fourteen, he learned his trade by hauling coal around the British Isles and eventually gained sufficient station to buy a share of a commercial sailing vessel, dubbed the *Williams*, since all three co-owners shared that first name. In 1812 William Smith began a series of voyages on his ship that took him farther and farther away from England's green and pleasant lands. Lisbon and Bordeaux were his first ports of call, then north, all the way to Greenland. By late 1818 he was making his fourth voyage to South America, an eighty-five-day sail from the Thames to Rio. With a cargo manifest that makes the *Williams* sound like a floating department store—cottons, silks, apparel, wrought iron, hats, iron, cutlery, saddles, musical instruments, music, books, wine, and confectionery—Smith sailed on from Buenos Aires to Valparaiso in Chile.

Along the way he made an unexpected detour.

The *Williams* had left Buenos Aires in January 1819. After it passed to the east of the Falkland Islands, winds made it impossible for Smith to round Cape Horn, the normal route to the western coast of the continent. So he sailed south, deeper and deeper into uncharted waters, and on February 19, after plunging through gales, sleet, and snow, he discerned in the distance what he thought was "land or ice." One can imagine the dark-complexioned Smith putting down his spyglass, blinking his eyes, and looking again—and yet again—before deciding that the dark mass on the southeast horizon was "so distinctly different (in) appearance . . . it must be land." The next morning he sailed closer and saw the profile of what appeared to be a large island, the dark outlines sketched on the horizon reaching far to the west. He was tempted to navigate the treacherous, icy waters to get closer but decided against it for a reason any twenty-first-century small-business owner can relate to: insurance. "Fearing the return of blowing weather, he was deterred from approaching nearer," wrote one historian. "As principal owner of the brig, he was unwilling to endanger the validity of his policy of insurance, in case of meeting with any accident in his research." No doubt with visions of soaring premiums in his head, Smith returned to Valparaiso. When he arrived there in March and reported his discovery, he was met with disbelief. Land that far south? Nonsense. Everyone knew there was nothing down there, just a sea of ice that had stopped even the great Captain Cook decades earlier. Surely icebergs were what Smith had seen, the silly bugger. "All ridiculed the poor man for his fanciful credulity and his deceptive vision," noted one contemporary account. Smith, though, "was not to be easily laughed out of his own observation. He had learned to distinguish land from icebergs."

Determined to visit these new lands again and verify his sightings, William Smith left Valparaiso for Montevideo in May 1819. This was now the southern winter, and the conditions were treacherous. It took him a month to reach the same latitudes, and when he did, he suddenly found himself hemmed in by ice. The skipper immediately hauled north, and the *Williams* broke free—although the ice ripped several sheets of copper off its hull in the process. He sailed back to Montevideo without finding land. What he did find on his return were some Americans very eager to talk to him. They had heard about his first voyage and, in particular, his observation of "a great abundance of seals and whales" in the waters near the land he had allegedly spotted. They offered Smith "large sums of money" to guide them to these islands. The United States was in full fur and sperm oil frenzy at the time; there were huge profits to be made, and these merchants were determined to make their share. But, wrote Smith himself in his "Memorial," or testimony, some time later, "having the good of the country at heart, [I] resisted all the offers from the said Americans."

Instead, he took his own vessel south once again. In September he sailed from Montevideo and, after fourteen days, passed Cape Horn, where he bore south-southeast. At 8 A.M. on October 16, he spotted land. He sailed closer, and this time there was no doubt. The next morning he continued southeast and saw what appeared to be mainland. "The land was very high, and covered with Snow, vast quantities of seals, whales, Penguins, etc. about the Ship," Smith wrote in his testimony. He continued along the coast until he found a suitable harbor. There he dispatched a landing party, under the command of his first mate, which planted on the beach a board with the Union Jack and what was described as "an appropriate inscription." With "three cheers," the crew "took possession in the name of the King of Great Britain." Smith decided to call the island "New South Britain." But "as that title, it was suggested, might lead to confusion with other places, Mr. Smith changed its name to New South Shetland, on account of its lying on about the same latitude as the Shetland Islands."

Smith and his crew were the first men to set foot on what we now call Antarctica. What they thought was mainland was actually a chain of what would eventually prove to be nine major islands lying off a peninsula that stretched for hundreds of miles into the then-unimaginable vastness of the southern continent. The largest of these islands, the one that Smith had come back to discover in the name of his sovereign, would come to be known as King George Island. One of the members of Smith's party described its barren and inhospitable nature. "There is not a tree, not a bush, not a shrub, not a flower," he wrote.

Having spent six weeks exploring the new land and mapping 160 miles of coast, Smith felt his job was done. Back to Valparaiso they went. There Smith reported his discoveries, presenting maps and drawings of what they had seen to a Royal Navy captain, who prevented Smith and his men from contacting the shore—"giving rise," wrote historian A. G. E. Jones in his book *Polar Portraits*, "to the rumor that a discovery of great importance had been made." The navy then chartered the *Williams* to return yet again to the new lands, with the purpose of ascertaining whether it "was an island or part of a continent, to take possession on each quarter of the land," and "to observe the character of the inhabitants." Of course, there were no inhabitants to observe, unless you count the animals—all of whose numbers would be decimated by the rapacious sealers and whalers, Americans mostly, who, despite the British attempts to establish ownership, would descend over the next few years on what we now call simply the South Shetlands. On King George Island and other places, they would perpetuate what to our modern eyes appears another form of madness.

▲   ▲   ▲

On the evening of February 24, 2005, the announcement came over the *Vavilov's* loudspeakers that we were approaching King George Island. As usual, we all clambered outside on the deck to see. Although the island is large—fifty miles long, fifteen miles wide—there was little to make out in the darkening gloom. However, we were about to send our own landing party—Gilligan and a handful of others were heading to the island to prepare for the marathon, which would take place in two days. They would stay overnight at the Russian base (ironically, there is no longer an official British presence on King George Island) and spend the next day marking the course with cones and flags, which, it was hoped, would not be carried off by skuas, as had been the case in the past. In the meantime we would do some South Shetland island hopping.

As if they were commandoes on their way to Normandy to soften up the defenses before D-Day, we wished the landing party well and promised to see them in two days as they skirted into the night. Afterward we gathered around the bar as one of the Peregrine staffers—world traveler, photographer, and world-class raconteur John Rodsted—told us a story that, he promised, would be about "bin Laden's balls." (The balls referred to turned out to be a brand of candy sold in Afghanistan, basically M&Ms for the mujahideen.) To prove there were no hard feelings between us over that seal and whaling business in the 1820s, I had an ale with Francis and some of the Brits. They had never heard of William Smith and were more interested in talking with me about American politics, a topic with which they seemed to be surprisingly familiar. Francis asked if I thought Condoleezza Rice or Hillary Clinton would be running for president in 2008.

The next morning I woke abruptly—and, as usual, smashed my head on the low ceiling of the cabin as I attempted to rise. The voice of Andrew, our expedition leader, was coming over the ship's speakers with an important message. "Good morning from the bridge," he said. "We thought you'd like to know we're about to pass through Neptune's Bellows, the entrance to Deception Island, our first destination today." I looked out the porthole to see, in the distance, a vast brown rock streaked with white protruding from an ice-speckled sea. We were in Antarctica! William and I scrambled out of our beds and threw on clothes. I helped push his chair over the various protuberances on the deck, and out we went into the chill air and dazzling sunlight of an Antarctic morning. Now that we were in the Shetlands, the waters were calm and the turbulent currents of the Southern Ocean and Drake Passage were behind us, so we could stand easy on deck and watch as we approached the ring-shaped island.

Deception Island, so named because it hides one of the safest natural harbors in the world, was discovered by another forgotten figure in the early history of Antarctic exploration, this one an American. Nathaniel B. Palmer of Stonington, Connecticut, was only twenty years old in 1820 when he sailed his forty-seven-foot ship *Hero* into Antarctic waters in search of fur seal. Some believe he would later become the first man to see the Antarctic mainland. Deception Island became a haven for the sealers and whalers. What makes the island either chilling or inviting, depending on your view, is that it was formed by a volcano that has been active as recently as the early 1990s. The volcanic activity below the surface has warmed the waters of its seven-mile-wide harbor to the point that on some days you can swim here (as participants in previous Antarctica Marathons have done). On the other hand, I thought queasily, it also meant that we were now sailing into the caldera of an underwater volcano.

First, however, there was the matter of getting through Neptune's Bellows, which sounds like the kind of ridiculous name you would hear in the cartoon *SpongeBob SquarePants*, where all the inhabitants live in Bikini Bottom and eat Crabby Patties. But navigating the Bellows, an opening into the protected harbor less than a thousand feet wide, is a serious challenge for a large ship. Very often the captain himself will take over the wheel of a vessel approaching the Bellows, because the margin of error is so low. Given what we'd heard about our captain—Leonid Sazonov, a veteran of the Soviet merchant marine—I suspect he could do it blindfolded. Sure enough, we squeezed through, 800-foot-high cliffs towering over each side of the ship. As usual, this was accompanied by a chorus of clicks, whirs, and beeps from the camera-wielding passengers—a veritable "ice-arazzi" who captured every Antarctic moment, following the movement of every whale and penguin as if they were red carpet celebrities on Oscar night.

After a hasty breakfast we clambered aboard the Zodiacs the way we had been shown during a brief lecture. With everyone encumbered in hoods, balaclavas, flannels, and a Land's End outlet store's worth of winter gear, we lined up by the gangplank; the Zodiacs had been lowered into the water and lined up alongside the ship. Jack did a double take when he saw William and me. "Ah, yes, William," he said. "Why don't you and your friend wait over here?" We moved aside and watched our fellow runners step gingerly down the gangplanks into the Zodiacs, which roared to life and whisked them off to the island. Finally it was our turn. Now came the tricky job of lowering a man with paralyzed legs and his wheelchair down a narrow gangplank into a small boat in Antarctic waters. With very little help from me, William rose out of the chair and managed to guide himself down, holding the railings for support. Despite his slight appearance, his upper-body strength was enormous. Meanwhile two of the Russian crew carefully, even tenderly, it seemed to me, carried his chair down behind us and placed it in the Zodiac next to us.

Off we went, the motorized rubber boat slicing through the waters of Whalers Bay. In the distance I could see glints of orange and red as our fellow passengers wandered around the beach. I, too, had dressed for Antarctica. Yet despite my snazzy Gore-Tex suit, expensive Gore-Tex gloves, and high-tech Gore-Tex hat, I was freezing. Apparently the one thing my friends back home had neglected to get me for my birthday was a Gore-Tex body. When we arrived, I stepped into several feet of water and slogged onto shore. (*Well*, I thought, *at least the Home Depot boots worked.*) The crew lifted William and the chair out of the Zodiac and onto the beach, which was covered with pieces of slatelike rock. He could barely get the traction to even move the wheels of his chair, so he sat motionless on the beach, contentedly admiring the scenery and the chinstrap penguins, which were curiously eyeing him (they'd never seen a wheelchair before). "Ho, ho," laughed William, who seemed to be enjoying the simple fact that he'd made it this far. "Don't worry about me. You go ahead."

So I wandered off to explore Deception Island.

It's no surprise that early visitors to the South Shetlands made this sheltered place a base of their operations. It stayed that way for decades, even after the Americans and Brits had moved on to other hunting grounds. By World War I there were thirteen whaling factories there, most of them operated in the austral summer season by the Norwegians. The remnants of some of these stations remain. I wandered past a storage building, tilted to its side and seemingly on the verge of collapse, that was guarded by a seal. (Don't get too close to them, we were warned; they weren't friendly.) Nearby, a cluster of rusting storage tanks stood mute in the stark landscape—brown, more brown, with a few streaks of white. That was the color scheme of this part of Antarctica.

While we consider this an uninhabited continent, that's not entirely true, at least on Deception Island. Over the decades men have lived, worked, and died here. A cemetery near Whalers Bay, where we had landed, contains the graves of thirty-five men, mostly Norwegian. According to a study of these graves by the Scott Polar Research Institute, almost all died in the years between 1908 and 1931. The ages at death ranged from sixteen to fifty-six; the causes included everything from cancer to beriberi (strange, one would think, to die of a "tropical" disease in Antarctica). There were also drownings and one poor seventeen-year-old mariner whose death was described as "opening boiler door by mistake." In 1969 a volcanic eruption melted the glacier above the graveyard and a thick roof of sludge collapsed on it, burying all the men again. One grave is still visible, a simple cross for a Norwegian seaman. This, I thought, was surely the loneliest grave on Earth.

After a couple of hours spent wandering the island—and yes, although I was too preoccupied with the graveyard and ruins to see it, a few brave souls took dips in the water—we returned to the ship and sailed out of the harbor into the open water. Next up was Half Moon Island, crescent shaped and just over a mile long. It's the site of an Argentine naval base and home to a vast assortment of chinstrap and gentoo penguins and Weddell seals. En route, we were summoned to the mess for an Italian buffet. This was our version of a prerace pasta party and a reminder that the next day was the marathon, a fact that increasingly occupied my thoughts.

As with every meal on the *Vavilov*, the Italian buffet was sumptuous. Still, as I inhaled forkfuls of capellini, I was worried. After slipping, sliding, and crunching around on the slate of Deception Island, I began to wonder what the conditions would be like on King George Island. One thing was certain: this was going to be painful. Every marathon is, to some degree or another, but when you start talking about rocks, as well as mud, hills, cold, pissed-off seals, dive-bombing skuas, and God knows what else, you're compiling a true twenty-six-mile itinerary of agony. My fellow passengers seemed oblivious to this as they laughed and chuckled at the cute gentoo penguins waddling around them, *oohed* and *aahed* some more, and checked off each type of seal on the master list Ziggy had distributed.

Later, back on the ship, I took my constitutional around the deck—good to stretch the legs—and bumped into a friendly young Irishman named Justin Lawson. Within minutes we were talking animatedly, not about the marathon we were about to run but about Irish and American history, topics we were both passionate about. I had been to Belfast and knew a fair amount about the Troubles. He had been to the United States and knew a lot about the American Revolution and the Civil War. We filled in each other's gaps. When the talk moved on to the polar explorers, Lawson proudly brought up Tom Crean, an Irishman who had sailed with both Scott and Shackleton and who is considered one of the strongest, most stalwart men ever to go south. His stamina and ability to work in the cold, not to mention his sunny attitude in the most horrid conditions, were legendary. Crean, too, had a connection to the South Shetlands. Yet like William Smith's, the Irishman's story, until recently at least, has been overlooked.

Born in 1877, Crean joined the Royal Navy at age fifteen. In 1901, while stationed in New Zealand, he was chosen as a last-minute addition to the crew of Scott's first expedition. Crean was twenty-five at the time and is described by his biographer, Michael Smith, as "a cheerful looking soul, with dark brown hair and clear hazel eyes. His trademark was the broad welcome grin and a warm open face." Physically strong, with a barrel chest and bricklayer's shoulders, he was never one to shy away from hard work or question an order, another reason his officers liked him. Crean would comply with any command happily, often belting out a tune, even when he was being ordered to "man-haul," the brutal method of transportation that the British stubbornly insisted on using in the Antarctic. This involved teams of men being harnessed like oxen and used to pull sleds loaded with hundreds of pounds of equipments for hundreds of miles across the ice. (The Norwegians, by comparison, disdained man-hauling and instead relied on dogs and cross-country skis.)

On Scott's two-year *Discovery* expedition, Crean spent 149 days man-hauling, a remarkable display of endurance and strength in what his biographer calls "the most physically demanding form of travel anywhere on Earth." Having distinguished himself on that expedition, he was promoted to petty officer. When Scott organized his return trip to the Antarctic, this time with the purpose of reaching the South Pole, Crean was one of the first men he sought out. This was the man you wanted when things got dicey, as they often did for those who were exploring the Antarctic. On that fateful 1911 trip aboard the *Terra Nova*, Crean was part of the eight-man team that made the "race" to the pole. But 146 miles from their goal, Scott announced the four men who would join him on the final leg. Crean, his crewmate and equally stalwart friend William Lashly, and Lieutenant Teddy Evans were sent back. While it was a bitter disappointment to Crean, he displayed heroic efforts during the brutal 750-mile march by the so-called "last supporting party." Famished, nearly frozen, the group finally had to stop thirty-five miles from help, when Evans could no longer continue. Lashly stayed with the officer, and Crean continued on a solo march, reaching the expedition's base at Hut Point after eighteen hours. Thanks to Crean, Evans survived.

Scott, however, did not. Historians have debated whether his doomed polar party might have made it home had Scott chosen Crean and Lashly as part of the five-man team. As it turned out, Crean was in the rescue party that found the bodies of Captain Robert F. Scott and two of his comrades the following season.

Crean returned to Antarctica a third time, in 1914—this time accompanying fellow Irishman Ernest Shackleton on the epic *Endurance* expedition. Things went badly almost from the get-go.

Their ship was trapped and crushed in the ice before it could even begin its polar exploration. After a desperate winter on the ice, the crew took to the lifeboats and made a run for Elephant Island, a gloomy outpost of the South Shetlands. They set up camp on the strand of beach below the island's forbidding dark cliffs. From there, Shackleton made the decision to relaunch one of the boats in search of rescue. Their hope lay on South Georgia, a subantarctic island about a thousand miles away in the South Atlantic. Crean accompanied Shackleton and four others on this famous, last-bid gamble. They crossed the Southern Ocean in the twenty-three-foot-long open boat, enduring, in the words of one writer, "plummeting temperatures, debilitating seasickness, a severe lack of drinking water, ferocious storms and mental anguish." In an incredible feat of navigation by Frank Worsley, they reached the coast of South Georgia—only to find that they would have to hike over an unexplored mountain range to get to the small Norwegian whaling village on the other side of the island. It seems inevitable that Crean would be at Shackleton's side as they and Worsley humped over the mountains to safety while the rest of their weary crew waited on the beach. The three exhausted mariners became mountaineers by necessity—and the first men to cross the ice-capped peaks of South Georgia. This last part of the *Endurance* saga became a sensation, in part because of the uncanny sense, felt and articulated by Shackleton, Crean, and Worsley, that they were guided by a fourth person. This "fourth person"—whether higher power or hallucination—inspired T. S. Eliot to immortalize them and him (or her or it) in his poem *The Waste Land*.

Crean came home in time for both World War I in Europe and the Easter Rebellion in his native Ireland. He remained in the Royal Navy, serving with distinction before retiring with honor in 1920. Still, the idea of an Irishman who had spent his life in service of the British might not have been well received during that tumultuous time in his homeland, so he stayed out of the spotlight and spoke little of his Antarctic heroism. In addition, Crean was a naturally modest man; hence, his relegation to footnote status. He did, however, open a pub in his native town of Annascaul, on Ireland's Dingle Peninsula. He called it the South Pole Inn, and he and his wife ran it successfully until his death in 1938. It is still a working pub today. When Crean died, Teddy Evans, by then an admiral and a lord, sent flowers. According to biographer Smith, Evans never forgot the humble Irish sailor who had saved his life, and he kept Crean's photo on his mantelpiece for the rest of his life.

Discussing all this with Justin, it occurred to me that Crean was the true endurance champion of Antarctica. He had done it in harness, he had done it on foot, he had done it by boat, over glaciers and mountains, while hungry and cold, and under the command of very different men. We modern marathon runners were coddled and soft by comparison. No fast young stud of the twenty-first century could out-heart Crean. Jason agreed, and smiled as we concluded our impromptu salon on the deck of a ship. "We'll meet at the South Pole Inn for a drink someday," he said.

Now that, I said, sounds like a plan.

Somehow talking about Crean bucked me up. He had endured, and he hadn't had any Italian buffet to fortify him. So what was my excuse? Whatever it was like tomorrow, I would get through it.

The ship was now heading back to King George Island, where we would anchor for the night in preparation for the race. Almost a century after having been largely abandoned following the seal and whale slaughter, King George was a hopping place again. In the years after the Antarctic Treaty was ratified and every signatory nation wanted an Antarctic station to call its own, this island on the fringes of the continent—accessible from South America and with a fine natural harbor—became the place to be. Now there are eight year-round and four summer bases here, and with a summer population of about five hundred people, King George Island is often called "the capital" of Antarctica. As opposed to the friction William Smith found among the British and American sealers and whalers in the 1820s, the various nationalities on King George Island today seem to work well together. Certainly this was true for the marathon—a welcome event on this remote outpost. Gilligan had spent the night on the island as a guest of the Russians. He returned to the ship after dinner to deliver our race instructions. Considering the busy day he had ahead of him as race director, he was upbeat. "Everything's great," Thom proclaimed. "I can't believe it's going this well." He was referring principally to the favorable weather, which had been with us all the way through the Drake Passage and now into Antarctica. No bitterly cold temperatures, and none of the snow squalls or turbulent seas that had vexed earlier editions of this race. So on race morning we'd breakfast at 7 A.M., and begin departing for the island at 8. There we'd meet the other runners for the race from our sister ship, the *Ioffe*—I'd almost forgotten there was another ship involved.

"The course will be marked by orange flags," Thom explained, and then went on to describe our 26.2-mile route. He referred to it as a double out-and-back. Starting at the Russian base of Bellingshausen, we would run 3.5 miles, through the Uruguayan base and up Collins Glacier to the turnaround point on the top.

Then back to Bellingshausen. From there we would run about 3 miles to the Chinese base, called Great Wall, and back again to the Russian base. That added up to 13.1 miles, meaning that those doing the full marathon (which was most of us) would run the entire course a second time.

Thom fielded some questions from the audience. One runner asked, what was the best way to attack the course? "This is a fat-burner's race," he replied, using the term that describes a pace when runners are going slower and longer, their bodies metabolizing more fat than carbohydrate, the primary fuel that powers the body in distance events. In other words, he was saying, keep your pace under control. "You'll die hard on this course by trying to run too fast."

Then he went over the water bottle system. At marathons in major cities, organizers provide the fluids. Long tables laden with water and Gatorade are set up periodically along the race course, usually every mile, and volunteers are there to hand cups of fluids to the passing runners. Not here. The Antarctica Marathon is self-serve. In the great Antarctic tradition of "laying depots" (creating storage areas for food and clothing), we would be laying fluid depots along the course—basically, our own water bottles, left in piles at a couple points. It was up to us to bring our own—and find our own. Yeah, yeah, I thought as Thom explained. I was still thinking about the course. Not the double out-and-back, which had confused me anyway. Thom had talked about glacial runoff; there had been mutterings from some of the Peregrine staff about the effects of global warming being evident on King George Island—receding glaciers and so forth. The weather conditions were good, sure, but no one had said anything about the conditions of the surface we were running on.

Back in our cabin I went through the ritual of laying out the race-day outfit I had carefully assembled through gift certificates and generosity: my super-soft base layer, the Craft zippered top, polypro pants, gloves, Runner's Edge ski band, sunglasses, and, of course, my worn-only-once Saucony trail shoes, which I put in the tote bag I would take to the island (we had been told to bring a change of shoes as well as clothes to wear after the race). Also, I decided to pin my race number onto the leg of my trouser now. Why start the next morning by drawing blood—particularly my own? As I did this, William—whose special, "glacier-ready" racing chair was already stowed away on a Zodiac—again pored over my book on Scott and Amundsen. I wanted to tell him about Crean and Smith, the "other" Antarctic heroes, as well, but I was too tired. At around 9 P.M., I climbed up into my bunk and fell asleep. I dreamed of sailing ships appearing on the horizon.

▲ ▲ ▲

Sometimes it seems that the history of Antarctic exploration is a continuous line, as straight as some of those plotted by Edward Bransfield, the skilled navigator who was assigned to the *Williams* on Smith's fourth voyage south, in December 1819. With the backing of the Royal Navy, they could now fully explore and map the new lands. Once in Antarctic waters, Smith, Bransfield, and the *Williams* crew of twenty-three spent ten days exploring the South Shetlands and became among the first men to see the towering mountains of the Antarctic Peninsula. This was the last moment of glory for Smith, the man who had, for all practical purposes, discovered Antarctica. Like Columbus, he had reached the island outskirts, not the mainland, of a previously unknown continent. Unlike Columbus, he never got the credit.

Smith returned for one more trip south, this time to try to cash in on the fur and seal harvest. When he got back to King George Island, he wrote later in "Memorial," "to [my] surprise, there arrived from 15–20 British ships together with about 30 sail of Americans, & during the fishing season it was with great difficulty your Memorialist maintained Peace between Crews of the two Nations on different parts of the coast." In late 1821 Smith returned to England only to find that his two co-owners of the *Williams* had gone bankrupt. To help pay off their debts, the *Williams*—a ship that by all rights should be remembered with Scott's *Terra Nova*, Amundsen's *Fram*, and Shackleton's *Endurance* in the history of Antarctic maritime exploration—was sold and returned to its original and ignominious task of hauling coal around the British Isles. Smith moved to London and worked for a time as a river pilot, but fell on hard times. In a deposition in 1839 he was described as "greatly reduced by age and infirmity" and was subsequently sent to an almshouse, where he died in approximately 1847.

By that time Nathaniel Palmer, the young American who had discovered Deception Island, was finding far greater profit as the prosperous owner and captain of a clipper ship. A portion of the Antarctic Peninsula is named after him (his house in Connecticut is also a museum). Palmer had met Bransfield, whose map—drawn during the voyage he took with Smith—was the first real glimpse into the great, long-rumored continent at the bottom of the Earth. A copy of that map eventually passed into the hands of Sir Clements Markham, who would become Robert Falcon Scott's patron. One of Scott's crew members Markham admired most was Tom Crean.

During that fourth journey by the *Williams*, a party from the ship landed again on King George Island and formally took possession of it. The date was January 22, 1820. Seven days later King George III died, and his son—who, as the prince regent, had been a sort of "acting monarch" during his father's illness—ascended to the throne, becoming George IV. At the time of his father's death, and in the years when those visiting King George Island could actually remember King George, the nature of his illness was unknown. To most it was just assumed he had "gone mad." In the 1970s researchers revisited his medical records and theorized that the cause of his so-called madness was a rare blood disorder called porphyria.

In the final moments of his life, as Smith and Bransfield were gazing out on the awe-inspiring sight of the Antarctica Peninsula, the king asked to be raised up, so that his sightless eyes could see . . . what? South, perhaps, to the far ends of the Earth, and a new world rising?

9

At a Glacial Pace

At the top of the glacier, I turned to look out over Admiralty Bay. Slivers of sunlight pierced the shroud of morning fog, revealing—anchored in glasslike green and blue waters—the two ships that had taken us from the tip of South America, across the Drake Passage, and into Antarctica. In the distance loomed the snow-white peaks of the South Shetland Islands, scattered off the tip of the Antarctic Peninsula, the twelve-hundred-mile-long arm that reaches out of the heart of the Last Continent.

It was a spectacular sight, but one I didn't have time to savor. I had to run—22.2 more miles, to be precise.

▲ ▲ ▲

After eight days and seven thousand miles, we were finally here. On a gray dawn, we rose aboard what had now become our floating home, ate breakfast (for me, the habitual hot cereal and bagel) and began the ritual, familiar preparation for a marathon in the most unfamiliar terrain. The evening before, we had listened to a lecture on what to do with our backpacks (leave them underneath the protective roof of one of the buildings on the Russian base), where to stash our water bottles (at two designated "water stations," about halfway through each of the two out-and-back loops), and what to do if we had to use the bathroom in the pristine and not-to-be-disturbed Antarctic environment (hold it in). I had listened to these instructions with one ear. Also, unlike some of my farsighted compatriots, I had chosen not to lug plastic squeeze-bottles of Gatorade—the kind easily obtainable at any 7-Eleven in the United States—for seven thousand miles, and so instead of a sugar-boosting energy drink, I was relying on water. "Good, old-fashioned water," I told William as were preparing to board the Zodiacs. "That's what got me through my first few marathons."

Of course, I was overlooking the fact that my first few marathons sucked; it wasn't until about my fourth attempt at 26.2 miles that I began to get the hang of it. And part of that involved sipping replacement drink along the way.

The Zodiac motored us across the bay toward the foreboding coast. King George Island in 2005 appeared to have changed little since the first description of the island was rendered in 1819 by a British official who had interviewed William Smith and his officers on their return to Valparaiso. "The coast was barren and rocky," wrote the official, who later published his account in a British magazine. "The land was high . . . the highest points being covered with snow, particularly the peak of a very lofty hill. At the place of landing, the spot was barren, stony, not of rounded pebbles but of bluish grey slaty [sic] pieces, varying in size from very large to very small."

As we got closer, I saw, rising out of the morning mist, something that hadn't been there in 1819: Bellingshausen, the Russian base named after that country's great nineteenth-century Antarctic explorer, Fabian von Bellingshausen, a guy who had been around when Smith and Bransfield were offering their description of the island. Bellingshausen, the station, truly gave me the sense that this was not just another island—it was another planet. The base, which hugged the shoreline as if prepared to make a quick getaway, looked like what a martian or lunar colony might resemble, particularly if that colony had suffered from serious financial reversal. It was a drab patchwork of buildings on stilts and round structures that looked like Antarctic porcupines, with antennae, satellite dishes, and other protuberances emitting from their round bodies. And incongruously, on a nearby hill, a lovely Russian Orthodox church—one of the few permanent structures in Antarctica and no doubt a source of solace for those in this lonely and wild place. Except for the church, only a year old, the rest of the base was weather beaten and bruised; it seemed to bear the weary resignation of post-Soviet Russia on the walls of its prefab buildings.

We had been warned about this by some of the expedition crew: there were nine bases on the island, some shiny and sparkling new and others that appeared as if they had been abandoned, if not by their crews, by their country. However, looks could be deceptive down here, we were told by the Peregrine crew. Don't judge the quality of either the functioning or the research done at these bases by how bright the coat of paint is. At Bellingshausen the shabby demeanor was offset by some crisp race-day operations. On the beach all was organized bustle. "Hello, hello!" cried a beefy Russian crew member in English as he helped pull our Zodiac on shore. "Welcome to Bellingshausen. Good luck in the race!" We marched a few yards onto the shore over to one of the buildings, dropped our bags under the shelter of a wooden ledge, and made our last-minute preparations.

It was an overcast morning but not especially cold, about thirty-seven degrees. This caused some consternation among several of the American runners, mostly Sun-Belters, who had come clad like Eskimos. Now they were realizing they would be overdressed. Imagine getting overheated in Antarctica. But it could easily happen on a day like this. As for me, the long-sleeve T, pullover, and pants I wore seemed the perfect ensemble for these conditions. For once, I thought smugly, I had dressed correctly for an occasion. I mentally thanked Bob Cook, the owner of my local running apparel store back home, who had helped select my outfit. For the first time in days, the passengers of both ships—the entire field for the seventh edition of the Antarctica Marathon—were together. That was good, but it also presented a little problem for the race organizers. To conform to an International Association of Antarctica Tour Operators regulation that prohibited groups of more than 100 visitors at any one point at any one time, the field of 212 runners—140 men and 72 women—had to be started in two groups.

One of the runners on the start line near me was Darryn Zawitz, a lanky thirty-five-year-old commercial pilot from Pittsburgh. He was mildly chagrined by the weather. "Temperatures in the 30s and not much wind?" he recalled thinking. "Heck, I'd run Chicago in worse conditions than that. So I mistakenly figured other warnings we had received about the race would be equally far off." Those warnings had included tough footing, steep hills, and dive-bombing skuas. These, too, Zawitz concluded, could be discarded as myth.

At precisely 9 A.M. the women, half marathoners, and men over sixty started; the rest of us took off over three minutes later. To the scattered applause of race organizers and curious base workers clad in red thermal coveralls, we went charging into ankle-deep mud. We represented fifteen countries, with participants' ages ranging from eighteen to seventy-one. There were students and surgeons, accomplished competitive runners and casual joggers; about ten staff members from the various bases ran the half marathon. "I was shocked at the range of people," said Stephanie Becker, thirty-nine, an ophthalmologist from Manhattan who sailed down on the *Ioffe*. "It was nice to see that the adventure spirit transcends age, nationality, and socioeconomic status."

I suspect, however, that during the very first moments of the race we all had the same self-doubts, as the insanity of what we were doing was quickly driven home. I had been expecting mud, but this was ooze so thick that it felt as if I were being sucked back into some primordial, microorganic previous life. Each step was slow motion, exaggerated, as if we were in some sort of tug of war with the island's surface. "Jesus!" said one runner near me, as the mud drew him in. "What the hell . . . ?" cried another. "It was up to my calves at some points," recalls Zawitz. Splish, splash, squish, splatter. Barely a quarter mile into the race, I felt the effort, the flash of fatigue and discomfort, my body's way of saying "uh-oh," and right there I knew.

This was really going to suck.

I slogged along, hugging the narrow ribbon of trail that linked the bases. My initially aggressive pace—somewhere I had nursed the far-fetched idea that I might be one of the top finishers in the race—had slowed. Now I was four miles into the 26.2-mile marathon.

After the fields of mud, we sloshed through some frigid glacial streams, and then we hit the glacier. Collins Glacier, we were told, was its name. But names mean little in Antarctica and especially on King George Island, where according to one survey there are more than a thousand officially registered place names for approximately 620 geographical features. Part of this is a result of the international cast on the island; the same ridge or bay might have both an English and a Spanish name. Plus there are many unofficial names, which, I suppose, Collins Glacier must be, since the only official Collins Glacier I could find on the continental map was on the western coast of the Antarctic mainland. So how about if I just refer to it as "the big, steep, smushy glacier"? Because that's how it felt. Decades of global warming had made the ice even slushier. It was like running up the side of a Slurpee mountain, one mushy, ice-crackling step after another. Because the slope of this half-mile-long ice giant was too steep to run—about a seventeen-degree incline—we had to clamber up, like human slash marks, bodies angled forward, arms pumping.

Miraculously, I felt better at this point, strong enough to pass a runner near the top of the glacier, a moment that was caught by race photographer Jim Boka, and that I am proud to show off in my album (as opposed to the photos taken of me later in the race, where I looked ready to collapse, and which I threw out). My spirits were buoyed by that move; we circled a cluster of orange flags—the turn-around point—and then, after briefly admiring the view, whoosh, we descended the same steep slope in what seemed like a barely controlled free fall. I had the odd feeling that I was a car motoring downhill with its parking brake on, and I half expected to see sparks flying off the heels of my now-soaked-in-ice-over-mud shoes. My new Sauconys—the same pair that had performed so well on the frozen trails of New Paltz—were as useless as Hush Puppies here.

Smack! We leaped off the glacier at its base and onto a field of scree, an insidious mixture of loose rock and stone common in Antarctica. I wobbled momentarily but managed to regain my balance and gingerly continued on, trying to skip my way across the slippery rocks and the rivulets that flowed through them. Daniel Powell, an Ironman triathlete from San Diego, was not so fortunate. He turned his left ankle on that same patch of rock and was reduced to a limping walk for the rest of the race. Yet he bravely managed to finish. "I thought about bowing out, but I'd never dropped out of a race before, and I wasn't going to do it here," he said later. The undulating landscape of the barren island opened up before me. There are no trees on King George, no vegetation, just patches of moss, some shallow, cold streams, and that seemingly endless supply of mud, made even mushier from the glacial runoff during this unusually warm Antarctic summer season. There were also hills that I began to hit with alarming frequency on my way back toward Bellingshausen, steep, muddy hills, a seemingly endless procession. The good feelings I had at the top of the glacier had melted away. I was struggling until I got to the rise of one hill and looked down. There was William, his scholarly mien twisted into a rictus of teeth-baring determination, his thick black gloves shredded from the effort of pushing the studded mountain-bike tires he had mounted on his wheelchair.

He was stuck, flailing with his arms. Dan, the other writer on the trip, who was assigned to do a magazine profile on William, was behind him, valiantly trying to push his subject out of the quicksand. "John!" said William. "Help!" I stopped. So did Jim

Lawrence, the son of a retired Marine Corps drill sergeant who was also running the marathon. As we tried to gather around the chair to help push, both Jim and I felt ourselves sinking, although not as fast as William. "It was scary," Jim said. "It seemed for a minute he was going to completely submerge into the mud." While I was flailing around trying to get my footing, the other two got their backs into it and managed to free William from the clutches of the ooze. Gritting his teeth, William continued on his painstakingly slow course across the island.

Because of the double-out-and-back layout of the course, runners kept passing one another. Dennis Martin ran by, looking determined and wearing an NYPD long-sleeve shirt. I saw people from the other ship that I'd forgotten about since Buenos Aires. There was Charles from Charlestown, walking. He didn't recognize me. Our time together in Buenos Aires just a week earlier seemed like a memory of years ago. Some of the race crew scooted by on ATVs. I saw a smiling face and raised hand of greeting behind a helmet and visor. It was Gustavo, here on what was probably his tenth trip to Antarctica, warm and cheerful as he was in the hotel banquet hall. Then there were the occasional people none of us knew, a reminder that King George was, by Antarctic terms, the bustling capital of the continent. Off a side trail, at one point, stepped a young man and woman in brightly colored thermals. He had what looked like a satellite dish protruding out of a backpack. They appeared to be scientists and paid no attention to me shuffling by as they intently studied the ground. Mudologists, I suspect.

While those two were preoccupied with their work, many of the base workers on King George Island were delighted to see us. For them the marathon was a welcome diversion from their lonely lives in the Antarctic. Nobody was more enthusiastic than the Uruguayans; a group of about twelve stood alongside the road near their base, waving their white-and-blue-striped flag and cheering wildly for each runner. As I passed them, I summoned up what little breath and Spanish I had. "*¡Buenos dias, amigos!*" I shouted. They roared in approval.

Humans weren't the only life forms we encountered in this alien environment. I saw a Weddell seal lounging on the nearby beach. A trio of gentoo penguins waddled across the road by the Chilean base. Meanwhile, the cold-eyed, black-beaked Antarctic birds known as skuas hovered overhead, keeping a watchful eye out for any runner that might get near its nests, hidden amid the hills. At one point, as the gluey Antarctic mud was beginning to suck the energy out of me, I looked up to find myself staring into the cold eyes and black beak of one of these big, nasty, gull-like predators. The skuas are known to attack those who get too close to their nests, which apparently I was. He hovered. I cowered. "I'm going as fast as I can!" I shouted to him, as I ran off, my body suddenly responsive to the threat of becoming skua supper.

By now I was hurting and thirsty. I saw people sucking on the Gatorade bottles they had left at the unattended water dumps, and I eyed them enviously. My bottle was muddy and looked as if someone had stepped on it. Like a man in a French Foreign Legion movie, alone and desperate in the desert, I needed a drink. As I stumbled past the water dump at about mile fifteen, I had an idea. Looking around to make sure no one was in sight, I grabbed the nearest and cleanest-looking squeeze bottle of Gatorade, held it a half inch from my mouth, and squirted down a few cold, delicious mouthfuls before carefully replacing it on its pile. Cackling maniacally, I continued.

Shameful, wasn't it? But this is what Antarctica had reduced me to—some sort of replacement-drink predator, rummaging through a pile of plastic bottles. Still, while I felt the sugar spike from the liquid, it didn't last. Soon I was dragging again, and I was not alone. The runners around me looked haggard as well. Later one of my shipmates on the *Ioffe*, Ron Bucy, from Bridgeport, West Virginia, would call this "the hardest marathon course I've ever done." He ought to know—he'd run 122 marathons in his life.

This was my twentieth, and as I began my second ascent of the glacier, I was almost sure it would be my last.

In his classic book on the sport, *Running and Being*, Dr. George Sheehan included a chapter about marathons, entitled simply "Suffering." In it Sheehan invoked the words of the philosopher William James to help describe what motivated marathoners and what they endured over the course of 26.2 miles. "[James] believed in effort. He thought the decisive thing about us was not intelligence, strength or wealth," Sheehan wrote. "The real question posed us is the effort we are willing to make." Testing that effort required what he called "a moral equivalent of war." Like war, Sheehan said, "this [effort] would provide a theater of heroism, an arena where one could demonstrate courage and fortitude, a setting where one could be the best one would ever be. For me and others like me, that is the marathon."

I think Sheehan was right. However, the problem for me was that while I was running a marathon—particularly this marathon—I felt no courage, no fortitude, no sense that I was at my best. On the contrary, as I forced myself up the glacier a second time, my chest aching, my legs burning, my head spinning, I thought that I had never felt worse in my life. Again I clambered up its steep and seemingly endless side, this time looking less like a human slash than a sagging, hunched question mark. Questioning, with good reason, just what I was doing here.

I was descending into a state that Sheehan described (later in that same "Suffering" chapter) as going "deeper and deeper into a cauldron of pain." The second time I reached the top of the glacier I was scratching the bottom of that cauldron. I circled the flags without bothering to take in the view. I may have even forgotten there was a view. I was slack jawed, body slumped over. Again, I scrambled over the scree, remarkably not falling. Again, I dragged my body up and down the muddy hills. And finally, at one point nearing the last turn-around, after a lengthy internal debate over the matter, I permitted myself to walk, a cardinal sin in marathon running—after all, you want to say you "ran" the marathon and mean it—but I was beyond caring. This is usually about the point in a marathon where the question "why?" is raised. *Why?* you ask yourself. *Why am I doing this?* That question is compounded in Antarctica, because you really didn't have to come all the way here to put yourself in extreme pain. Agony is easily available in our day-to-day lives if we want it, right? (As Woody Allen might say, just invite a life insurance salesman into your home for the evening.) So with so many normal ways of inflicting pain on myself, why was I doing this, here? Our springy tendons and other anatomical advantages; our Greek tradition of running; my interest in visiting a place few others would. None of those explanations cut it out here, when my anatomy was aching and my spirit soured by pain. So, again, why? Why were two hundred of us doing this? Why had dozens more ended up on a waiting list, eagerly awaiting the chance that they might do this?

Benjamin Cheever mulled the *why* question in his 2007 book *Strides: Running Through History with an Unlikely Athlete*. Cheever recalls once foaming about writing to another writer, Nuala O'Faolain, telling her while he didn't much like other writers, he did like all the runners he knew. "Of course, you love each other," she replied. "You're all high as kites." She was referring, of course, to the legendary "runner's high," which some believe is the effect of those oft-discussed endorphins or other brain chemicals (others say it may just be a response to increased blood flow or merely that people are more relaxed when they run). Regardless of the physiology behind it, Cheever's point is that we run to feel good. I think he's right, up to a point—and that point, I had now reached. Any endorphins or "feel good" chemicals that had flooded my body at the start had long since slid off me like sweat. Any intellectual theories by guys from Harvard that I was doing what I was meant to do because of humanity's superior anatomical design were overwhelmed by the proletariat cry of working muscles that were demanding time off immediately and, for all I knew, might even be preparing for a work stoppage. And as for the idea of me doing this because nature intended it—well, nature never intended me or anyone else in my species to set foot, much less run, here in Antarctica, and nature was now making that point clear by kicking my ass.

At this point I promised myself that I would never do another marathon again, here or anywhere else for that matter. At this moment I wanted nothing more than to return to society, or at least that part of society that offered hot showers, warm beds, and cool pints of ale.

Without any possible reason or rationale to offer, other than just wanting to finish the damn thing, I kept going. At this point in the marathon, sights and sounds became impressionistic, which is another way of saying that I was delirious. I remember a Chinese staffer at the Great Wall base, poking his head around a corner and peering at me curiously from underneath his cap as I came plodding by. By the Chilean base I almost stopped in my tracks when I saw a child—a little boy dressed up in a parka, big mittens, and boots. With most of the oxygen at this point going to my legs, my mind seemed to be on low power and things took a longer time to process. I was already well past the parents and child, as my mind, like a laptop computer whose batteries are running slowly, painfully framed the interior question.

Why . . . kid . . . here?

Later I would learn the answer. As part of Chile's assertion that the South Shetland Islands are really an extension of that country's territory, Chileans wanted to show that, unlike other nations, their presence on these islands is not limited to scientific research and temporary seasonal staffs. They, the Chileans, actually have a community here, with families and a school (the children, I was told by a Peregrine staffer, are on King George Island only during the Antarctic summer, however).

A few miles ahead of me, Zawitz, running alone and in the lead, was feeling just as bad as I was. "The entire second half of the race was misery, pain, and determination, in equal parts," said "Zawi," who had marveled at the view from the glacier the first time on the top ("It left me in awe") and had cursed it the second ("That stupid pile of ice"). By the last couple of miles he, too, had been reduced to painful jogs of a few hundred yards, interspersed with walking breaks. But when he saw the finish line, he managed to pick it up, crossing the line "with my head held high and arms in the air, in true champion style." He had won the 2005 Antarctica Marathon, in a time of three hours, forty-nine minutes, about an hour slower than his normal result. This was something new to Zawi; although an outstanding runner, he had never won a race. "It was a little surreal," he said. "No cheering crowds, no finisher's medal hung around my neck. Just a few folks from the ship to pat me on the back."

After some more mud-trudging, I mustered up the determination to jog again. What motivated or shamed me was the thought of Crean and Shackleton at the end of their epic journey, hiking across the mountains of South Georgia. They had their "fourth man," that spiritual presence each sensed walking beside them, giving them strength. I really couldn't convince myself that any higher power would invest a moment to help me in this bizarre, self-inflicted miasma of pain. Just then, however, I spotted on the crest of the next hill, my fourth man. Her name was Annie Hotwagner, and she appeared well on her way toward being skua supper when I caught up with her at one of the self-serve water stops at around mile twenty-two. She looked peaked, exhausted. "I got vertigo, pounding across those rocks," she said. Hotwagner, forty-three, from Saugatuck, Michigan, was running to raise money for Memorial Sloan-Kettering Cancer Center, helping to fight a disease that had claimed the lives of many friends and family members. A noble cause, but at that moment, however, she herself needed some support. I found some unexpected strength in myself. "Come on," I said, confidently. "Come with me." We fell into a ragged rhythm together, walking the uphills, then jogging back down for three miles. By this point our depleted bodies had left us with marathon tunnel vision: all we could see was the muddy road ahead. Hotwagner, however, was determined. By completing Antarctica, she would not only raise money for an important cause but also become a member of that exclusive Seven Continents Club. Antarctica is obviously the toughest "get" on that list—and Hotwagner was beginning to feel its effect. With a mile left, she began to fade. "Don't wait for me," she called. Too tired to be chivalrous or supportive at this point, I followed her instructions.

Later on, over a cup of hot tea in the ship's mess, Hotwagner, who finished four minutes behind me, would call it "the greatest physical accomplishment of my life." I would tell her that although she was struggling too, her presence, her company, our shared suffering the last few miles, somehow helped me continue running. And that was the truth.

I crossed the makeshift finish line at the Russian base with as much flourish as I could muster, spreading my arms out in triumph and smiling for the camera. Compared with the typical marathon finish line—loudspeakers, balloons, a band, hundreds, even thousands of spectators—this was pretty bleak. The most notable fixture was the signpost telling you how far various cities were (MOSCOW: 8,000 KILOMETERS, for example, or MINSK: 10,000 KILOMETERS). The problem was that the signposts were written in Cyrillic, so I couldn't even understand them. I was walking stiffly toward the baggage storage, where I would change out of my wet clothes and mud-encrusted shoes before being ferried back to the ship, when I heard Gilligan calling me. "Hold on!" he yelled, as the race photographer fiddled with his equipment. "The flash isn't working. Let's do it again."

I hesitated. Attempting to re-create one's finish in, say, the New York City Marathon—where up to 311 runners cross the line every minute—would likely result in disqualification or a fistfight. But heck, I thought to myself, this was Antarctica; the participants in this race are stretched out for miles. I jogged back out a few feet on the course and sprinted across the line.

Same arm spread. Same forced smile. Same result.

So, alas, there is no photographic proof that I completed the 2005 Antarctica Marathon in four hours and forty-two minutes—17th out of 176 finishers (another 36 completed the 13.1-mile half marathon). You'll have to take my word for it. So will Bob Cook. The running-shoe store owner who probably had hoped to see his logo caught in a dramatic finish line photo of me in the local newspaper would instead get a stammered, lame apology on my return (the good-natured Cook just laughed; I think he was surprised I came back at all).

As I wobbled over to pick up my bag, I looked down at my shoes. They looked as if they had been left overnight in a bowl of fudge brownie mix. I thought about how to dispose of them: Viking funeral, perhaps? Put them on a makeshift little raft, set the whole thing on fire, and push it out into the Southern Ocean? Hmm, I'd probably be breaking about a dozen international laws doing that and would spend the next six months washing dishes on the *Vavilov*. I was out of creative ideas. I was out of everything, in fact. Painstakingly, I pulled the soggy shoes off my feet, put on my dry boots, and wearily climbed a flight of wooden steps to the postrace aid station. I noticed that it had started to snow.

▲ ▲ ▲

William finished about a half hour later than I, after having gone half the distance. For my roommate, it was a day to forget. "I was so excited," he told me later. "Then . . . boom! It was mud and it got worse and worse." Although he had mounted knobby, mountain-bike-type tires on his racing chair, he began to sink into the muck. It took him fifteen minutes to go the first one hundred

yards. "I was horrified," he said. So was everyone else on the
course—many of whom had become as enamored with him as I
had. "I cried, watching him struggle," said Dr. Claire McGrath,
the race physician. But William hadn't gotten through medical
school by whining, and he wasn't about to do it here. "I kept thinking, *Things will get better.*" Gilligan, driving the course on an ATV,
knew better. Although Tan had come equipped with an ice ax to
drag himself up the half-mile-high glacier, unusually temperate
weather had left the ice soft and slippery. While most of the runners were able to clamber up and then run back down the steep
glacier, Gilligan turned Tan back at its base and told him he could
make up the distance at the other end of the two-loop course. "He
couldn't get past the loose rocks or the glacier," Thom said. "We
told him to try to go back and forth on the other loop, between
Bellingshausen and the Chinese base." Later Tan would chuckle
about all this, particularly his inability to hack his way up a soft
glacier. "I was defeated by global warming," he said.

More problems arose on the course: A screw came loose in
Tan's lead wheel, forcing him to abandon his racing chair for his
everyday chair, which he had brought along (it had the bigger
tire)—a move akin to a marathon runner changing out of his
Nikes and into his wing-tip dress shoes halfway through the race.
Then there was the ten-inch-deep, quicksandlike mud he had to
be rescued from. After a few hours it was clear he wasn't going
to be able to finish the course before sunset, so Gilligan and others convinced him to complete the half marathon—13.1 miles—
instead. Reluctantly, William complied. At the previous year's
Boston Marathon, he had completed 26.2 miles in one hour, fifty-
nine minutes, and fifty-five seconds. In Antarctica it took him five
hours to go less than half that distance. Still, William's effort

made him the star of the race. "I told him it was an honor to be on the same course with him," said Zawi. "To see him going inch by inch gave me strength," said Len Gibely, a runner from Massachusetts who was on the *Ioffe*. "It gave us all strength." Tan, who gave all he could give, made a believer out of Gilligan. After the race, he compared William's effort to Shackleton's. That famous British explorer failed in his 1914 attempt to cross Antarctica by foot, but through heroic efforts he eventually brought his men, including Tom Crean, back alive. "William didn't succeed in his original goal, but he modified his plans under the circumstances and managed to achieve something highly significant," said Gilligan. "He's the first and maybe the only wheelchair athlete ever to compete in Antarctica." William drew a slightly different parallel to Antarctic history. He had speed-read my book on Scott and Amundsen, and we had discussed how the British commander had stubbornly relied on the inferior methods of man-hauling and ponies to get him around in Antarctica, as opposed to skis and dogs, like the Norwegians had used. As William second-guessed himself over his whole setup—his tires (maybe they were too heavy for the mud), his racing chair (maybe it was too light for the terrain), his plan to hack his way up the glacier (the ice was too soft)—he concluded that he, like Scott, had been ill-prepared and humbled by Antarctica.

"I came with ponies," he said to me. "I should have brought dogs."

Not everyone was as serious in their suffering as Zawi, William, and I. Some of the back-of-the-packers actually had fun doing the Antarctica Marathon. They just slowed down, took their time, submitted to the mud, and tried to enjoy the bizarreness of the whole thing. In retrospect, they were probably smarter.

Della Works, a feisty sixty-nine-year-old from Casper, Wyoming—here because "I wanted to do these kinds of things while I'm still young"—and her friend, Nita Kay LeMay, the legally blind runner from Hawthorn Park, Illinois, soldiered on despite being near the back of the pack, which was soon strung out across King George Island. Walking most of the way, they didn't care about finish time (it took them just over eight hours) and were more interested in international diplomacy. At home LeMay works as a hostess in a Chinese restaurant. When she called out *"Kung hei fat choy"* to some of the workers at the Chinese base on King George Island, they acted as if they'd seen a polar bear. "Here's this white, blond-haired women running along and wishing them 'good fortune in the New Year' in Mandarin," she laughed. Once they got over their shock, the Chinese came over, chatted, and took photos with the two women.

Jim Lawrence's father Don, the retired marine, reckoned this was one of the most difficult things he had ever done ("only Vietnam was tougher," he said). Unlike me, however, Don decided to stop and smell the proverbial roses on the treeless island. "At the top of the glacier the second time, I decided I'd earned the view," he said. So he plopped down, pulled out a PowerBar he had carried along, and had a sort of brief, impromptu picnic on top of the glacier, gazing out over the water for a few minutes before continuing. "I was so inspired by the scenery and by just being in Antarctica," he said. "That's what pulled me through."

After crossing the finish line, I collected my bag and staggered up a rickety flight of steps to a sort of postrace gathering place inside one of the Bellingshausen buildings. In conventional marathons this would be called the "Family Meeting Area" and usually would include ample quantities of refreshments for the hungry and thirsty finishers—bagels piled high, boatloads of bananas, and tables of Gatorade. In the Antarctica Marathon it was more like a Russian MASH unit. In the corner I noticed another runner, lying on a cot, with an arm swung across his head. I sat down heavily on a stool as a red-flannelled medical technician asked me how I was doing. "I'd feel better if I could run up that glacier a third time," I joked meekly.

She looked at me with eyebrows raised. "What?"

"Just kidding," I said. "Do you have any Gatorade? I didn't bring any." (Yeah, plain old-fashioned water was all I needed . . . right.)

"Yes, here," she said, and handed me a large white packet and a cup of water. The packet was blank except for the words *Electrolyte Replacement Drink*. Ah, I thought, a real generic brand! Probably what they served in the Russian navy. With cold fingers, I shakily poured the powder into the glass and used a coffee stirrer to mix it. It looked foul but I was thirsty. I took a big slug and felt as if I had just swallowed a mouthful of ocean water. *Gaaaakkkk*. I spit it out all over the wooden floor. Either no one saw me, or no one said anything. I guess I wasn't that thirsty. Where was a 7-Eleven when I needed one, I thought?

Slowly I changed out of my wet muddy clothes and into my Gore-Tex suit. I was motioned back down the stairs and out onto the beach by one of the Bellingshausen crew members—the same fellow, I realized, who had welcomed us. "You finish? Good job!" he said. They were running Zodiacs from the beach to the ships, like shuttle buses, and because most of the runners were still out on the course, the boats weren't crowded. "*Vavilov?*" one of the beach masters asked me. "Right," I said, and plopped down next to Alyn Park. I was surprised to see her—a pretty but somewhat fragile-looking woman from Denver who had never been seen without her husband until now. "How did you do?" I asked. She looked a bit sheepish. "They told me I was the first woman." First woman! The women's winner of the 2005 Antarctica Marathon! That's huge! Not only that, but the delicate-featured Alyn was fifty-three—the oldest winner, male or female, in the race's ten-year history. I congratulated her, and the two of us sat shivering together as the boat skimmed across the water.

We arrived at the ship and clambered up the gangplank to the deck. As I walked toward my cabin I heard music. It was almost as surprising as seeing that child on King George Island. I realized I hadn't heard music in days. Listening closely, I recognized the tune . . . a driving beat, a soaring, synthesized keyboard phrase. It was "Heroes," the great David Bowie anthem from the late 1970s. Where was it coming from? I looked around and saw small speakers connected to a portable stereo set up by the entrance to the staff cabin shared by Ziggy, the naturalist. Of course Ziggy would be playing Bowie! While he was back on the island with the rest of the expedition crew, helping with the marathon, he had left his music here to serenade the returning runners. He had a continuous loop of Bowie songs being played, but somehow "Heroes" just kept going on and on. The song echoed down the hallway, filled my head, and took me away as I got back to my cabin, stripped off my clothes, and got ready to shower. I began to dance—a rare and horrifying sight under the best of circumstances, but even worse here. With just a towel wrapped around my waist and a pair of flip-flops on my beaten feet, I stumbled, creaked, and sashayed down the hallway, like a stoned eighteen-year-old at a concert, to the rhythm of the song. "*We can be heerrroes,*" I sang as the glorious hot water cascaded over me. "*Just for one day-ay!*"

As I washed the Antarctic mud from my body, I found myself thinking—between gargled attempts at singing along—about what we, all of us on that ship, had accomplished that day. No matter how offensive or ridiculous it may have seemed to some—an invasion of Antarctic sanctity, a self-indulgent exercise—the truth was that all of the runners here had the guts, the persistence, the temerity to travel seven thousand miles to the bottom of the Earth in order to run 26.2. They made it across the finish line, every one of them.

Did completing the Antarctica Marathon make us heroes? Not really, but it was nice to feel that way—just for one day.

10

BICYCLE-RIDING GRANDMAS OF THE ANTARCTIC

In retrospect, the story of the "Bicycle-Riding Grandmas of the Antarctic" sounds like a Monty Python skit. You can imagine John Cleese, Terry Jones, and Michael Palin, in drag and screeching at one another in faux-feminine Cockney accents. But it was true and a delightfully bizarre postscript to our edition of the Antarctica Marathon. Shirl Kenney, seventy, of Cedar Rapids, Iowa; Joan Irwin, seventy-two, a New Yorker at the time (she later moved to Lead, South Dakota); and Sharlene Anderson, fifty-six, from La Verne, California, met while doing an around-the-world bike odyssey in 2000. There, as they rode an average of eighty miles per day through forty-five countries and six continents, Kenney, Anderson, and Irwin—who between them have seventeen grandchildren—forged a friendship that would be rekindled a few years later, when Anderson decided she wanted to run Antarctica.

Around the same time, Kenney happened to be in Los Angeles, near Anderson's home, on a flight layover. They met for lunch at the airport. Anderson told her about Antarctica and impulsively added, "Wanna come with me?"

Kenney's immediate response: "What a crazy idea! I would love to!" When she got back to Iowa, Kenney quickly recruited Irwin, then living in New York. They hatched a plan: the two elder women would act as Shar's "support crew," and, of course, they'd all get the rare privilege of seeing Antarctica. I met them over breakfast in Buenos Aires; it turned out that I had written about Irwin, who was living not far from me on Long Island, for *Newsday* when she returned from that around-the-world trip. The story, which appeared on the cover of our feature section, attracted the notice of a producer at the Regis Philbin show, who booked Irwin for a segment. She rode out to the stage on her twelve-speed, wearing her bike helmet, as the audience (and Regis and Kelly) went crazy.

Over lunch in Buenos Aires, the grandmas told me jokingly that they'd ridden bikes on every continent except Antarctica. "Now at least we're going to get to see it," Joan said. Why not ride it, I asked? "John," she said to me, her eyes narrowed. "We didn't bring our bikes." Oh, right. Still, I thought it was a great idea. Gilligan disagreed and dismissed it out of hand when I brought it up to him. It was against regulations. Besides, he and his group had been granted permission to run a footrace on King George Island, not some stunt involving bicycles. I forgot all about it after that, but the grandmas apparently didn't. Kenney, in particular, kept the idea in the back of her mind as they sailed through the Drake Passage on our sister ship, the *Ioffe*, where they delighted the rest of their shipmates. "They were well liked," says

Kal Bittianda, a runner from Manhattan who also was on the *Ioffe*. "Definitely characters . . . risk takers with no lack of spirit."

That spiritedness was proven on race day. As Shar ran along the muddy trails, Shirl and Joan volunteered as course monitors, helping to point runners in the right direction. Assigned to a point near the Chilean base, Shirl—who had not forgotten our conversation in Buenos Aires—began asking everyone she saw whether there was a bicycle available. Finally, an English-speaking man in a military uniform said there was. Because families stayed on the base during the Antarctic summer season, he explained, there was a child's bike at the base gym. "My eyes widened," Kenney said later. "I asked, 'how do I get permission to ride it?' And he said, 'I give you permission.'" With the blessing of the officer, Kenney made a beeline for the indoor gym. She found the little bike mounted on the wall, lifted it off, and rode up and down the adjacent forty-foot-long corridor for about ten minutes. Then, she rushed off to tell Irwin. Meanwhile, Anderson was getting near the finish of the marathon. With about a quarter mile to go, she saw her two friends excitedly calling her on the course. "Come back when you're done! We've got something to show you!" Too tired to argue, Anderson trudged back to the gym after crossing the finish line (in six hours and forty-two minutes). When she saw the bike, she was reenergized. After taking her brief turn riding up and down the corridor, Anderson said, "I felt like the three of us had done something extraordinary."

Irwin had a slightly different reaction to her five-minute ride on the seventh continent. "It was a bit of a lark," she said. "But it *was* a bike ride!" Anderson added. And so what if the Guinness Book of World Records wasn't there to document it? "I don't really care that it's not official. We've done it and that's what counts."

As the grandmas were riding in circles around the gym, I had showered and headed up to the communications room of the ship. In 2005 there was still limited e-mail access to Antarctica, and only satellite phones worked. The *Vavilov* had one, and everyone was welcome to use it if he or she didn't mind paying something like fifty dollars a minute, which I didn't, if only to let my wife know I had survived the Passage and the marathon.

"How was the weather?" she asked, her voice distant.

"Not bad," I replied. "Thirty-seven degrees at the start. Got a little colder as the day went on."

Donna laughed. "It was twenty-two degrees here today. So you're telling me it was warmer in Antarctica than New York." There was silence; then she asked in a concerned voice, "Is that normal?"

Good question. The Antarctic Peninsula is often called the most rapidly warming place on Earth. And it's true that over the past few decades the air temperature has risen six times as fast here as the rest of the Earth and several major ice shelves have collapsed. There is anecdotal evidence as well: even such veteran Antarctic travelers as Gus, Thom Gilligan, and the Peregrine crews said that in just the course of a decade, they had noticed changes—the glacier on King George Island seemed to recede, its ice softer and the ground wetter. But the more scientists study the changes here, the more puzzled they are. For example, meteorological observations have found that only in the western part of the peninsula, and only during the winter season, are the temperature changes really exceptional. Other studies suggest that current trends, such as the decline of penguin populations on King George Island, mirror events in the past and may be due less to climate change than to migratory patterns. This isn't some knee-jerk, head-in-the-sand denial of global warming or its dangers. It's simply recognition that whatever is happening isn't simple. As one paper concluded, "A complex interaction is underway [in the Antarctic Peninsula], one that involves climate warming, air and ocean circulation changes, sea ice retreat, and melting of land and shelf ice." Clearly, though, something is happening—and as ice shelves continue to tumble into the sea at this writing, that something does not bode well for the future.

Of course no one was complaining about the heat in the mess hall of the *Vavilov*. The drop in temperature over the course of the day, our wet feet, and the chilly ride back across the water had all left us craving warmth. Around a late lunch table I sat, across from shell-shocked-looking fellow finishers, some of whom had come directly from the Zodiac to eat. We talked in muted tones about the glacier, the rocks, the mud. One person who didn't seem to mind the conditions was Ingrid, the tough British army officer. I had seen her at the turnaround, far closer to me than her modest prerace predictions would have indicated. As the group around our table dug into yet more plateloads of pasta, an escalating war of words ensued. We tried to describe just how bad we felt and how tough it was on the island: "Awful" . . . "God-awful" . . . "Horrible" . . . "Horrific" . . . "The worst . . ." Adjectives exhausted, the group fell silent. Ingrid piped in, "I didn't think it was so bad." You could have heard a soup spoon drop. All eyes trained on her, and she squirmed a bit uncomfortably. "Er, at least I didn't think it was . . . *that* bad." How, I asked her, could anyone say that running on King George Island was anything but diabolical? Where else on Earth could one encounter such conditions? Ingrid cleared her throat. "Well, up in the midlands, I run in this kind of stuff all the time." More incredulous stares. What stuff was she talking about? Were there glaciers in Birmingham or Coventry? She shrugged. "Mood," she said, with her accent. "I run in mood all the time. It's very rainy in England, you know."

It was hard to argue with that. We decided there and then that to properly prepare for the Antarctica Marathon, in the age of global warming and glacial runoff, a runner just needed to be in the right mood.

That night there was a bit of a "drink-up," as Francis called it. He, the Rocket Scientists, Ingrid, Amanda and I sat at the bar, raising a few glasses to our success. I don't remember much of it, not because we had that many toasts, but because I was fully toasted already. It was an early night, and so exhausted was I that I didn't even need to do my middle-of-the night, bump-bang-scrape-stagger to the bathroom.

The next day was the most perfect, greatest, most wonderful day in the history of Antarctic touring, at least if you believed the peppy language of the daily log, posted early every morning by an unseen hand in the cabins of the *Vavilov*. "We woke up to the breaking of clouds and calming of winds," read the entry for February 27. "Soon into the day the sky was almost free of cloud and clutter—Antarctica in its full glory. It was a day of perfect photos of ice-capped islands, towering crags, continents domed in ice, icebergs, and amazing wildlife."

Actually, it was a day for me to be blue, even in the face of such unshakable cheerfulness. Something happens after the marathon, a kind of postpartum depression that represents the crashing low after the soaring high of completing 26.2 miles. Flushed with brain chemicals, or maybe it's just relief, I'm on that high for the afternoon and evening following a race. After completing the New York City Marathon in 1987, I partied "like it was 1999." I took ten people, including my future wife, out to dinner at a swank restaurant, bought rounds of drinks afterward, and couldn't understand when no one else wanted to join me for a nightcap at 1 A.M. The next day everything looked and felt bad, and it wasn't just because of the hangover or muscle soreness. The same thing was happening here, a long way from New York City. Part of it, quite frankly, is that I had expected a better performance. I was used to running times in the low three hours and even accounting for the difficulty of the course and conditions, I had still envisioned myself finishing strong, certainly not sucking wind and walking for much of the last few miles.

I'm usually a glass-half-full kind of guy. But on the morning after the race, the glass was lying on the floor in pieces. Doug Kurtis, a former elite U.S. marathoner, calls the condition "postmarathon depression" and says it's a common phenomenon among runners. "The excitement of the marathon is over and the intensity of preparation is behind them," he writes in the *Detroit Free Press*. "The sense of focus and purpose is lost."

My spirits were buoyed, however, when I strolled, a bit gingerly, on deck to find out that we had left the South Shetlands and were headed south. The *Vavilov* was now approaching the Antarctic Peninsula, the mainland of the continent. On the night of February 27, we sailed through the Gerlache Strait, and on February 28 we prepared to land on Danco Island. These are important names in Antarctic history, linked to another of the great sagas of polar endurance. Unlike those of Scott and Shackleton, however, this story is largely forgotten today—in part because it was such a mess.

In 1897, five years before Scott's first expedition, Belgian Royal Navy officer Adrien de Gerlache led an international crew south. In addition to men of his own country, there were also Norwegians, Russians, a Romanian, and an American on board—two of whom would become significant figures in polar exploration. Because its mission was primarily scientific—another first—the *Belgica* was a floating laboratory replete with the latest in scientific technology. One of the best and brightest of the scientists on board was Emile Danco, a young Belgian geophysicist. The man who would have the biggest impact on the voyage—and also the last member to join the crew—was a thirty-two-year-old physician from Brooklyn. Dr. Fredrick Cook had been part of an American expedition to the Arctic led by Robert E. Peary in 1891. After unsuccessfully trying to organize his own Antarctic expedition, Cook settled into private practice in the Bushwick section of Brooklyn (his house still stands). In August 1897 he read an item about de Gerlache's expedition in a New York newspaper. We may suppose that a number of patients went untreated that day, since Cook immediately sent a telegram volunteering to be ship's doctor on the expedition. De Gerlache, whose original choice for ship's physician had dropped out at the last minute for "family reasons," responded with equal swiftness, telling Cook to meet them in South America. That was end of the private practice: Cook packed his bags, said good-bye to his family, and booked passage for Rio de Janeiro. The good doctor was positively giddy about the prospect of seeing Antarctica. Going there, he wrote later, had "always been the dream of my life, and to be on the way to it was then my ideal of happiness."

Taking on Cook turned out to be a good decision by de Gerlache, one that may have saved the expedition.

The *Belgica* first explored the South Shetlands, lands that had been largely ignored by explorers in the half century since Smith,

Bransfield, and Bellingshausen. They continued south to find new islands off the part of the Antarctic Peninsula called Graham Land. The deeper into these still-unknown parts of the continent they went, the thicker the ice became. Despite warnings from his crew and the scientists to turn around, de Gerlache persisted, almost as if he wanted to get stuck in ice when winter arrived. "Although there was no sharp dissent," wrote David Thomson in *Scott, Shackleton, and Amundsen*, "it was a situation not unlike that facing Columbus. Neither the bold nor the cautious knew what risks they were taking."

Soon the *Belgica* was stuck in ice, and de Gerlache and his crew were forced to endure the Antarctic winter—the first time a crew would be iced in through the long, dark polar night. They were poorly prepared and, it seems in retrospect, poorly led. There was little organized activity for the men, who soon grew listless and sullen, particularly after the sun disappeared entirely on May 15. Even more problematic were the food supplies. The *Belgica* was stocked primarily with tinned meats, cereals, biscuits, and macaroni; it was short on fresh fruits and vegetables and the as-yet-unrecognized vitamin C. Before long the crew was showing signs of scurvy.

As the days in darkness mounted, Cook noted how the men's faces became puffy and oily, their ankles and eyes swelled up, and their skin grew over their fingernails to protect them from the cold. Conditions deteriorated further, and on June 5, Danco—who had supposedly suffered from heart problems in the past—died. He was not yet thirty years old. It seemed that the rest of the crew wouldn't be far behind. With the combination of inactivity, constant darkness, and poor diet, some crew members were even said to have gone "insane."

Cook knew the symptoms of scurvy. During his expedition to the Arctic a few years earlier, he had become fascinated with what were then called Eskimos, and as a medical man he was particularly interested in how these native peoples managed to avoid the dreaded disease while subsisting on a diet devoid of vegetables and fruits. "Cook surmised that the large amounts of raw or barely cooked fish and meat the Eskimos ate must provide some benefit in preventing scurvy," wrote his biographer, Howard S. Abramson.

Based on his study of the Eskimos in Greenland, Cook told de Gerlache he had a solution to the dietary woes: fresh meat from seals and penguins. The leader protested. The meat from these creatures was oily and distasteful, he argued. But eventually, when Cook found an ally in the first mate, de Gerlache gave in. The crew was fed fresh meat, their strength improved, and when warmer weather returned, the *Belgica* was freed from the ice and headed back home. By at least one account, Cook was the real hero of the expedition. "He of all the ship's company was the one man of unfaltering courage, unfailing hope, endless cheerfulness, and unwearied kindness," wrote the *Belgica*'s first mate. "Not only was his faith undaunted, but his ingenuity and enterprise were boundless."

The future would not be so kind to Cook or his reputation. A decade later he returned to the Arctic and in April 1908 claimed to have reached the North Pole. This was disputed by Peary, who reached the pole a year later. A long, bitter public feud began that would involve scientists, newspaper publishers, the National Geographic Society, several Eskimos, and even the Congress of the United States. In the end Cook was discredited and Peary declared the first man to the top of the world, a position he still occupies today in history books. What exactly happened here? Was a charlatan exposed, or was a decent man the victim of character assassination by a jealous rival? That depends on which camp one was in. Cook later became an oil speculator, got caught up in the Teapot Dome scandal of the 1920s, and went to prison, which certainly didn't help his reputation. Although both men have been dead for decades, the controversy over Cook and Peary lives on. There are competing societies, books, and Web sites that still argue, often with astonishing hostility toward each other, as to which of these men reached the North Pole first and who deserves the accolades.

One of the few people who stood by the disgraced doctor during his travails was the first mate of the *Belgica*, who had by then established himself as a great explorer in his own right and whose successes were achieved in part by avoiding some of the mistakes he saw on de Gerlache's expedition—and applying some of what he had learned from his American friend on that same voyage. Whatever Cook did or did not do later, this man knew that the doctor's service on the *Belgica* had been exemplary and said as much, even though he knew that by doing so, he would provoke the wrath of the powerful Peary lobby. He didn't care and stuck by his old friend, visiting the disgraced physician in federal prison in the 1920s.

The name of Cook's old shipmate and lifelong supporter was Roald Amundsen, the first man to reach the South Pole.

▲ ▲ ▲

When it came to sustenance on the *Vavilov*, no one was going to suffer from deficiencies of anything except restraint. On February 28 we wolfed down the usual sumptuous breakfast and climbed into the Zodiacs to visit the island named in honor of the *Belgica*'s young scientist. Danco Island is a penguin rookery and the site of much activity—1,573 pairs of breeding gentoos were counted here in a 1991 survey. While we happily did not witness any gratuitous penguin sex (or at least any that I would have recognized), the curious creatures were all around us as we trudged up what had been billed as a hill but felt to me like an icy mountain. Through white mists and sprays of snow we climbed, following the tracks of the penguins until we reached the top and could see across the strait to the spectacular mountains along the distant coast, also named after Danco. (Didn't anybody, I wondered, think about naming something after Cook?)

Most of my fellow marathon travelers were not nearly so silly as to concern themselves over a finish time in Antarctica. A number of them, however, were eager to expand their marathon portfolios, some of which were already vast. At dinner after the climb, Francis introduced me to Roger Biggs, chairman of the London-based 100 Marathon Club—an organization for those who had completed at least 100 marathons. Roger was already up to 315, a mind-boggling number. However, he had bones to pick, primarily with Gilligan's Seven Continents Club. Biggs, who declaimed loudly over dinner that night about this, objected to the criteria used to define the continents. I asked for an example. "Aw-right," he replied, in his marvelous Cockney accent. "'ere's one. Ha-wah-e. If you run the Honolulu Marathon in Ha-wah-e, that counts as Nawth America." He paused, waiting for that to sink in, and then raised his voice several decibels. "You cawn't tell me Ha-wah-e is in bloody Nawth America!" He had a point, I admitted. But one of his fellow Brits then posed this question. "Okay, fair enough. But if Hawaii doesn't count as North America because it's not part of the mainland, can running London count as Europe?" The geographical debate raged on as I discreetly left the table.

The next day we sailed through the Errera Channel and into Andvord Bay, on the western coast of the peninsula. This was Antarctica the way we had all pictured it: white mountains looming over us, glaciers on a frozen march to the water, icebergs dotting the mirrorlike water. Seals and whales abounded, making the bay seem alive at some points. I had rarely seen such natural beauty in all my life, but it masked a dangerous reality. In 1922 two members of an English scientific expedition were stranded on Andvord Bay. They spent a long and harrowing twelve months there, and in their account, reprinted verbatim in the *New York Times*, the words *natural beauty* were never mentioned. Rather, the harshness of the conditions in even that relatively benign corner of Antarctica makes one shudder. "Few people can imagine the terrific force of an Antarctica gale," wrote T. Bagshaw, one of the two men. "The icy wind comes roaring down the mountains direct from the South Pole and sweeps all before it. Our hut would rock and tremble, threatening every moment to fall before the gathering forces of the storm." The two were eventually rescued, but looking out at peaceful Andvord Bay, a seal sunning itself on a small iceberg nearby, it was easy to forget how quickly things could turn for the worse here; and in the back of the mind that disquieting thought reappeared—that we really aren't meant to be here, running or no. Beyond this perfect and benign landscape lurks an indifferent fury that could simply sweep us away.

A different but, in its own way, equally sinister fury was stirred up that afternoon. The Peregrine staff announced that for two hours the ship store would be open. Immediately, quiet reflections on the vastness of our world and fragility of the environment were shattered by the rustling of American dollars. Step aside, you Aussies, Brits, and Asians! My fellow Americans and I raced down to the ship store, scarfing up *Vavilov* sweatshirts, hats, T-shirts, key chains, and beer mugs as if it were Black Friday at the local mall on Thanksgiving weekend. Particularly popular items were the bright red Last Marathon jackets and vests, which disappeared faster than Cabbage Patch dolls or Nintendo Wiis. People tried on, modeled, eyed one another's purchases jealously, and generally behaved with the conspicuous consumption that might be as much a part of the American genetic code as those springy tendons for running.

As I waited in the checkout line, I clutched an armload of souvenirs as if they were relics from Scott's hut, including two Antarctica mouse pads, a *Vavilov* sweatshirt and kid's T-shirt, a key chain, and two stuffed penguins. Astute readers will note that I have admitted in previous pages to not even really liking penguins. But, well . . . they were on sale.

The little shopping orgy was followed by an auction, where things like a copy of the ship's course chart signed by our captain and a book on Shackleton signed by his two daughters were sold to the highest bidder. This turned into a demonstration of another American favorite pastime—impressing everyone with how much money one has. The corporate execs and trust fund kids on the ship were the ones upping the ante, raising the bidding, while most of the rest of us sat in a slightly embarrassed silence. "It was strange," recalled Ingrid, who is British. "It was the one occasion that separated the group, into those with ridiculous money and those without. That was a shame. . . . Before that we were all runners and individuals with one aim." A total of five thousand dollars was raised at the auction and the money went to a good cause, the Save the Albatross fund, which also sounds a little like something from a Monty Python bit, except that according to Ziggy the albatross really do need saving. Still, Ingrid was right: there was something very ugly about this. In this pristine land, so carefully protected by treaty and consensus, we had briefly but essentially been members of a moneyless society. I hadn't touched my wallet or cash for a week. But now, near the end, we had managed to sully and tally it all up into the haves and have-mores.

One of the last highlights of the Antarctica Marathon cruise was the big sleep out on the glacier, overlooking Andvord Bay. The last time I had gone camping was when I was a Boy Scout. It had poured rain, my uniform and sleeping bag got soaked, and I got a twelve-year-old boy's version of diaper rash. I had no wish to repeat the experience. William and I stayed on board while about twenty-five of our fellow passengers, including the Rocket Scientists, went ashore. They were given a choice of tent camping or sleeping under the stars in a bivvy sack (a waterproof shell that covers one's sleeping bag). The Rocketeers, brave pursuers of the Final Frontier that they are, chose the latter. Before zipping his bag up, one of them, Mark Ferguson, recalled looking out over the bay and seeing the lights of the *Vavilov* glimmering in the distance. Then he fell into a deep sleep, only to wake up finding himself, his bag, and everything else around him covered in nearly half a foot of snow, far more than is normal for this part of Antarctica in the summer. "We were completely buried," he said. "But we weren't wet. These bivvy sacks worked." Mark, and the other two Rocket Scientists, Bill and Tim, loved it. Others didn't. One group couldn't take the cold, the snow, or the awful portable, leave-nothing-behind toilet nicknamed Mr. Yum Yum. At 3 A.M. they decided they wanted to go back to the ship. To do so, they had to wake up staff escort Jack, the craggily handsome buccaneer. Envisioning Jack sleeping with a cutlass at his side or a knife in his teeth, I would have thought twice before waking him up. These people went ahead and roused him—and they were never heard from again. No, actually he took them back and perhaps was happy to be back on board ship himself.

That was it, though. The sleepover was just that, over. "We didn't have any great party or a big snowball fight or build some giant Antarctic snowman," Mark said. "We just got up, dusted off the snow, and headed back to ship."

By the next day we were back in the Drake Passage. We spent most of the time watching movies and listening to lectures. One of the films was a great sea yarn about rounding Cape Horn in the age of sail. The documentary was narrated by a man who had actually sailed in the early 1900s and was still alive at the time the film was made. He talked portentously about himself and his fellow "sea dogs," being "whipped by the merciless wind," as grainy black-and-white footage of sailing ships being battered by storms flickered before us. It was good—so good that for the first time on the entire trip, I began to feel sick. Real life I could handle; it took a movie to send me lurching to the exit of the darkened auditorium. Once I got outside I was fine. I got out just in time to hear the announcement that we were in sight of Cape Horn itself. I rushed to the stern of the ship and there it was, in the distance, a giant rock rising above the empty horizon.

Again, the lyrics from an obscure rock song were somehow downloaded into my consciousness. A haunting and majestic 1969 ballad about the sea by the progressive rock band Procol Harum.

Across the straits
Around the Horn
How far can sailors fly?

How far, indeed? On our last night out, I sat at the bar next to Jack, who for once was not surrounded by adoring female passengers. I was told he had a background in oceanography, which I'm sure is true, but there was a well-cultivated air of mystery around him, hints of a past with dark secrets. Normally outgoing, he was reflectively subdued on this last evening of our voyage. He and his fellow expedition leaders would probably get a night's rest in Ushuaia before turning around to do one more journey back to Antarctica for the season; this one would follow a similar itinerary, except that the two ships would be peopled by bird-watchers, amateur photographers, or adventure tourists who weren't quite adventurous or motivated enough to want to run 26.2 miles. I asked him a bit about how his life had led him to this remote place. He looked up at me. "I once met the Dalai Lama, mate," he said. I must have looked skeptical. "No, really, we met him. And you know what he said to me?" I shook my head. "He said, 'Jack, you've been a bad man. You're condemned to sail the Antarctic for the rest of your life.'" And he smiled, ever so slightly.

The next morning I woke to Jack's voice, which sounded even fainter than it had in the bar. I thought I was dreaming at first, but it was indeed Jack, making an early announcement over the loudspeakers: one last invitation to imbibe with the merry Peregrine crew. "Good morning," he said, sounding almost dreamy himself. "The pilot is guiding us into Ushuaia. Join us on the bridge for tea and coffee as we pull into the dock." I scrambled outside. The sun was rising over the Beagle Channel, and in the distance I could see the lights of America.

Southern Discomfort, Northern Exposure

Shortly after returning home we learned that we'd heard the last of the Last Marathon. That name—chosen by Gilligan in 1995 because he couldn't believe his own audacity in attempting to organize a race in the Last Place on Earth—wasn't deemed sufficiently obvious for an event that now seemed to garner worldwide publicity every time it was held. Right after the 2005 race, the event became known as the Antarctica Marathon.

Another surprise: it was not the only one.

Less than a year later, in January 2006, a different 26.2-mile race was staged in Antarctica. This one was on the mainland of the continent. Called the Antarctic Ice Marathon, it was the brainchild of Irish ultramarathoner and adventurer Richard Donovan, who had successfully organized a marathon at the North Pole in

2003. In Donovan's view, Gilligan's Antarctica Marathon wasn't Antarctic enough. He wanted something on the continent's mainland, something where the temperatures were guaranteed to be cold, where runners would tread on ice, not mud, where the dominant color scheme would be white on white. He settled on an area called Patriot Hills, about seven hundred miles from the South Pole at an altitude of three thousand feet. In his marketing for the race, Donovan promised subzero temperatures and winds blowing up from the pole at ten to twenty-five knots. This was the Antarctica race for those who wanted to experience Antarctica the way Captain Scott had (well, except for maybe dying of exposure). Nature lovers were not encouraged to enter. "Forget about penguins or crowds cheering you along the route," he wrote on the Web site. "No penguins live this far south and you will have to rely upon yourself to push onward in the hushed, indomitable surroundings." The only form of deprivation that the Ice Marathon couldn't promise was seasickness. Since the competitors would fly on a cargo plane, four and a half hours from Punta Arenas, Chile, into the interior of the continent, there was no need for a ship.

Add to this the cost of about fourteen thousand dollars per competitor (not including airfare to Chile), and it's no surprise that the Ice Marathon attracted few takers—there were fifteen finishers in the debut edition. Still, they included some intrepid and marvelous characters. Among them was Donovan himself, the true "bi-polar" runner—a veteran of endurance competitions in extreme conditions at both ends of the Earth, in stark contrast to one of the runners who had signed up for his Ice event.

Mike Pierce hailed from the distinctly nonpolar environment of San Diego, California, but had always wanted to visit Antarctica. Pierce's problem was how to train for the subzero weather expected in the Ice Marathon. Having grown up outside Philadelphia, he knew well the 1976 movie *Rocky*, in particular the famous scene when the fighter played by Sylvester Stallone trained in his friend Paulie's meat locker. Pierce, then forty-one, realized that this might really make sense for him. "I picked up a phone book, and just looked under *ice*," Pierce recalled. It took him about thirty calls before he found somebody who didn't hang up on him when he explained that he wanted to run around like a hamster in one of their freezer compartments. Finally, he was given access to a massive, twenty-acre commercial refrigeration facility near the Miramar Marine Corps Air Station. "I asked [the owner] which of the boxes was the coldest," Pierce recalled. "He said, 'the one for ice cream.' I said, 'That's where I'm going.'" Box 9—where temperatures were kept at an average of minus ten degrees Fahrenheit, was only forty feet wide and sixty feet long. Pierce calculated that it would take him about 44 laps around the ice cream locker to cover a mile. Surrounded by giant palettes of Breyers and Baskin-Robbins boxes, he began to run around and around and around . . . and around . . . the freezer, eventually building up to a distance of twenty-six miles (about 1,144 laps). He also brought a stationary bike into the freezer and pedaled for hours with a giant industrial fan in his face to simulate the fierce Antarctic winds.

Pierce was dismissed by many as a good-natured nut, but what he was doing actually made perfect sense—acclimating himself to his environment and the task at hand. It worked. On race day Pierce, who was running in only his second marathon, took seven hours to go the distance, not unexpected considering that the granular ice of the polar plateau made for slow footing. The only problem, he said later, was his running outfit. Along with goggles, a face mask, and a head-covering balaclava, Pierce wore three layers of clothes, including a middle layer of fleece and an outer layer of Gore-Tex. "I was overdressed," he said with a laugh.

The zero-degree day of the Ice Marathon was about ten degrees warmer than the San Diego freezer.

Unlike a one-time South Pole Marathon held a few years earlier—a race that had, in many ways, been a well-publicized debacle—Donovan's Antarctic Ice Marathon was held again. In the second edition of the race, held in December 2006, Donovan added a 100K (62 mile) ultramarathon. Back to the freezer Pierce went, this time doing two runs of 50K (31 miles) in a fifty-nine-foot-wide locker. "I got blisters on the balls of the foot from all the starting and stopping before I hit the wall," he said. Again, though, his deep-freeze conditioning paid off, as he was able to finish the ultra in seventeen and a half hours.

Pierce's success on the ice has provided a frozen platform for a new career. A former sales manager in the insurance and recruitment industries, he now travels the country giving speeches and corporate sales training under the name "Antarctic Mike." In his presentations—through which he promises to "teach greatness to your sales forces"—he combines his sales knowledge with inspiring tales of Antarctic and polar history, plus his own marathon experience, to address "the key leadership issues that people and organizations face every day." (And no, the sessions are not held in an ice cream locker.)

In November 2006 the Antarctica marathon ante was raised even higher when a group called Racing the Planet added an Antarctic stage race—the Last Desert—to its series of events held in deserts around the world. Their rationale was that Antarctica, the highest, driest continent in the world, was indeed a desert. Fifteen adventure runners flew from Punta Arenas to King George Island, then took a private ship around the South Shetlands and the Peninsula, running stages on Deception Island, Cuverville Island, Neko Harbor, Paradise Island, and Aitchoo. The second edition of the island-hopping stage race, held in 2007, was interrupted partway through when the expedition's ship received a distress call from a cruise ship that had struck submerged ice and was sinking just off the coast of King George Island. The passengers were forced into those cramped and horrid lifeboats that Jack had joked about during our halfhearted drills on board the *Vavilov* in 2005. Those horrid boats, though, saved the lives of 154 people. The image of that ship, on its side in Antarctic waters, was broadcast all over the world and confirmed the worst fears of many who have worried about the growth of Antarctic tourism. (Fortunately all the passengers were rescued by two other ships.) The Last Desert event continued and was won by an American, Joe Holland, the first of eleven competitors to complete the 150-kilometer-long (93.2-mile-long) event. This time, though, there was no running on King George Island. "We won't stage anything on King George again," said Mary K. Gadams, founder of Racing the Planet. "We think it is too unattractive and very un-Antarctic-like."

When I heard this, a part of me felt miffed, almost defensive, about the muddy, wet, slushy course we had suffered through. "What's the matter?" I wanted to tell her. "You don't like beat-up old Russian prefab huts on stilts? Or melting glaciers?" Anybody can run around Neko Harbor, where you have all this fantastic beauty around you! It takes real toughness to sink into all that mood, I mean mud.

What's the point, though? She's right. No one has viewed King George as anything but barren and bleak since William Smith first peered at its shores through the mist, trying to figure out if it was an iceberg or land. Still, I'm proud to have completed the "Coolest Race on Earth." So are my fellow travelers, many of whom have continued their adventurous ways.

Jules Winkler—who helped instigate the marathon around the ship in 2001—went on coaching and competing around the world. In 2006, at age seventy-four, he traveled to Australia, and upon completion of the Gold Coast Marathon there, he became a member of the Seven Continents Club (which at this writing counts about 180 members). Fred Lipsky joined that exclusive club a few years earlier, by virtue of his completion of a marathon held on a game preserve in Kenya. The following year, however, he severely injured his lower back while trying to clear away debris at the scene of an automobile crash. The accident ended Lipsky's marathon-running career, at least for a while. In 2007 he retired from the police force, earned his certification as a personal trainer, and opened a gym on Long Island for older adults called Five-0 Fitness. He now wisecracks his way through supervised, one-on-one workouts.

Rita Clark of Green Bay, Wisconsin, also joined Seven Continents and is now about halfway through her goal of running a marathon in all fifty states. She's taking her time—about two marathons a year. "I have a long way to go," she admits. "But goals keep us focused, and what better way to spend retirement than running and vacationing?"

While still a long way from retirement, the Rocket Scientists continued to boldly go where few others have. In May 2007 Mark Ferguson and Tim Rumford were among 117 finishers in the

Tenzing-Hillary Mount Everest Marathon, which runs down from the Everest base camp, at 17,572 feet, to the Sherpa town of Namche, at 11,305. It took them a little over nine hours to finish a race that Ferguson called even tougher than Antarctica, because of the altitude. On July 12, 2008, all three Rocket Scientists were off again: Ferguson, Rumford, and Bill Wrobel completed the Knysna Forest Marathon in South Africa. This made six continents for the trio; Oceania is their last stop on the road to the Seven Continents Club.

In 2006 Darryn Zawitz joined David and James Ross, our father-and-teenage-son marathoners from Antarctica, on a lovely little jaunt called the Canadian Death March, a 125-kilometer (77.7-mile) race through the mountains of Alberta. "If you've never run 13.6 miles at night," Zawi says, "wearing a headlamp and safety glasses, on a single-track trail, with a gazillion tripping roots and rocks, with nothing more than tiny reflective dots as markers for the route, up and down massive hills, keeping an eye out for bears . . . I'd highly recommend trying it!"

Roger Biggs still serves as chairman of Britain's 100 Marathon Club—although he has long since exceeded that threshold. Since Antarctica, he has run a staggering 110 marathons, a pace of about 3 per month. Biggs completed his 429th career marathon, in Spain, in November 2007 and shows no signs of stopping any time soon.

Francis Staples ran in his hometown London Marathon in 2005 and 2006, as well as marathons in South Africa and Thailand, where, like the indefatigable English gentleman-traveler he is, he went elephant trekking in the jungle. In April 2007 he also became a bi-polar runner, completing Richard Donovan's North Pole Marathon. "I consider myself most privileged," he says, "at having visited both ends of the Earth." His recollections of the Drake Passage, King George Island, and the 2005 trip remain powerful. "How incredibly fortunate we were in 2005 to have enjoyed calm conditions and such scenic cruising," he says. He's also proud, as he puts it, at having "survived the Collins Glacier experience times two . . . and not forgetting the dive-bombing skuas, of course."

Ingrid Hall is living in Edinburgh. In 2008 she plans to participate in a rowing-trekking odyssey that involves sailing from the Falklands to South Georgia Island and then retracing Shackleton and Crean's hike across the mountains. "These friends of mine think I'm some kind of Antarctic veteran, because I've been there once," she said. Her friend Amanda Payne is still a practicing pediatrician and lives in Sussex. Unlike many of the others, her running has consisted of a couple of half marathons since 2005. She's had other priorities: Her twenty-four-year-old son recently survived a "short but terrifying bout" with cancer. Antarctica, she says, "seems like a lifetime ago."

A veteran of more than a decade of Antarctic travel, Thom Gilligan continues to return to the Last Continent year after year. The race was held for the eighth time in 2007, and of course he was there to help organize it. This time 188 runners finished the full and half, although unlike the balmy conditions of our race, they were blanketed by a late-summer snowstorm. "There was a stretch of the course when I could not see anything in front of me," said Michelle Johnston of Lake City, Minnesota. The thirty-three-year-old mother of four finished in 5:33:59. The winner of the race was Matt Tyler, also thirty-three, from Shawinigan Lake, British Columbia, who finished in 3:51:33. Christine Harding, thirty-one, of Weston, Maine, took the lead in the last two miles to win the women's division in 4:54:50. Behind them were the usual cast of inspirational runners, including Ginny Turner, fifty-four, a race walker from Hillsboro, Oregon, who was the last to finish (in 8:30:35) but the first woman to complete a marathon on all seven continents—twice. Jeanne Stawiecki, a fifty-six-year-old registered nurse from Charlton, Massachusetts, was attempting to become the first woman, and only the second person, to both run a marathon *and* climb the highest mountain peak on all seven continents. She finished the Antarctica Marathon in 5:22:08 and then finished her seven-continent quest a little over two months later, when she reached the summit of Mount Everest. Oh, and one more thing about Stawiecki—she was a two-pack-a-day smoker until her late thirties.

My former bunkmate, William Tan, returned to King George Island in 2007 with a modified racing wheelchair, but to no avail. The snowy conditions defeated his valiant efforts, and again he had to settle for finishing the half marathon, which he did in just under six hours. Eight months later, however, William was back for a third attempt in Antarctica, this time as a competitor in Donovan's Ice Marathon, which he finished in 9:48:32, becoming the first wheelchair athlete to complete a marathon in Antarctica and the first to complete one on all seven continents. The achievement, I'm sure, was somewhat bittersweet for William, however. Just two months before his great achievement, William's nine-year-old friend Jessica Doktor died in Children's Hospital in Boston following a bone marrow transplant. William loved that little girl, was inspired by her courage and cheerfulness in fighting cancer, and had dedicated all six of his Boston Marathons to her.

On August 29, 2007, another great loss, as Gustavo Papazian, the stalwart, good-natured Argentine and Antarctic veteran, died suddenly, apparently of a heart attack, in Buenos Aires. Gus, who had been on every Antarctica Marathon trip since 1997, was only forty-six years old. "I am heartbroken," Gilligan said when he relayed the news.

Gus will no doubt be sorely missed for many reasons, not the least of which is that in order to try to meet demand, the Antarctica Marathon is now being held annually. The 2008 and 2009 editions of the race were fast sellouts. Still, at this point in his career, Gilligan doesn't need to be sloshing around on glaciers and putting up course markers. He could be spending most of his time at his homes on Cape Cod and Maui. Why does he choose to put himself through the stress, discomfort, and sheer hard work of planning such an extraordinarily complex event every year? "I need something to keep my blood boiling and get the adrenaline going," he said. "It keeps me alive."

▲ ▲ ▲

Watching the 2007 Antarctica Marathon unfold from afar, I realized I, too, needed something to get the adrenaline going again. In March 2007 I completed the National Marathon in Washington, D.C. I did it in 3:12, a decent time for a fifty-two-year-old and sufficient to restore my status among my running partners on the bike path at home, who had looked askance at my slow time in Antarctica, mud or no mud. It wasn't until I got home that I noticed something startling in the results of the D.C. marathon: William Tan had finished six seconds behind me, and yet I hadn't seen him, hadn't even known he was in the United States, much less the race.

Passing like two ships on the Beagle Channel at night made me think about how far we had come in only two years. It also made me realize that, while satisfying, running in D.C. certainly wasn't an adventure. This, I suspect, is a problem for many of those who have run marathons in places like Antarctica, an experience singular enough to make even the tremendous excitement and energy of the major urban marathons almost ho-hum. Particularly for runners not interested in *fast* times (again, that term is relative), the lure of running the Great Wall of China, Mount Everest, the North Pole, the Bataan Death March Memorial Marathon in New Mexico, and, of course, Antarctica, the most remote race of all, is powerful.

How long will the call of these adventure marathons continue to beckon, or even fascinate? Ron Watters, a senior lecturer in outdoor studies at Idaho State University, says he thinks it's just a matter of time before interest begins to ebb. It has nothing to do with novelty, or terminal cases of shinsplits, and everything to do with generational cycles. Watters, who has studied the historic patterns of generations and the degree to which each is involved with the outdoors, found that periods of intense interest in nature and the outdoors are typically followed by decades where the focus is elsewhere. An example, he says, is the GI Generation of World War II, which followed two highly active outdoors generations. The so-called Missionaries (born 1860–1882) included Shackleton, Scott, Amundsen, and Fredrick Cook. And the Lost Generation (1883–1900), despite the interruption of World War I, produced, among others, Everest climber George Mallory and Kurt Hahn, the founder of Outward Bound, not to mention Ernest Hemingway. The GI Generation, by comparison, came back from the war and focused on building families and institutions. "Overall public interest in outdoor activity waned during this period," Watters notes.

He thinks the same thing is about to happen: the Millennials (those born between 1982 and 2004) will be far less likely to go running off to Antarctica than the Baby Boomers and Generation X–aged men and women before them. "Millennials will be busy facing and overcoming challenges of everyday life, and their time for outdoor experiences will be limited," Watters predicts. "Based on generational analysis we will see a gradual decline in interest and participation levels." So what does this mean for events like the Antarctica Marathon? "We will see a drop of interest as time goes on," he says. "Especially once the Boomers can't do these things anymore."

I can see it now—a ship full of octogenarian Baby Boomers heading to Antarctica to shuffle through what could truly be called, again, the Last Marathon, our own Viking funeral march on King George Island. Sign me up now.

There are other practical reasons that endurance competition in Antarctica may begin to tail off. Although some will no doubt try, it's hard to imagine other events that could be held there without provoking the ire of the international authorities or the scientific communities. A triathlon, for example, would require swimming and biking as well as running. Three grandmas circling the floor of a gym on a kid's bike is one thing; it's hard to imagine anyone giving permission for hordes of mountain bikes to go thundering down a glacier. Then again, with climate change and economic pressures, anything is possible. A sprint triathlon to kick off the grand opening of the South Shetlands Sheraton? Let's hope not, but who knows?

As for the long-term interest in adventure racing, studies of outdoor participation at this date, 2008, are already beginning to suggest that Watters is right. Participation in outdoor activities is beginning to decline after years on the upswing. Community service and technology seem to be emerging themes for the generation in ascendance. The Millennials, he says, "don't need to risk life and limb like some of the Gen-X-ers, nor do they need to escape to the outdoors like the Boomers."

▲ ▲ ▲

This Boomer, for one, still needed an adventure. After the National Marathon in D.C., I began combing the Web site www.marathonguide.com, looking for bizarre races. I found one in Finland with the unlikely name of the Santa Claus Marathon. It started on the Arctic Circle, at a popular European family tourist attraction called Santa Claus Village, and finished in the nearby city of Rovaniemi. What's more, the race was held in late June, at the time of the midnight sun, affording the unusual opportunity to run, sleep, drink, eat, and do anything else under the light of a blazing Arctic noon.

This was the marathon for me, I decided—or at least half of it. I wasn't ready to run another 26.2 miles so soon after the one in Washington, so I elected to do the 13.1-mile half marathon. The difference between doing something in the far south and the far north was striking. As opposed to all those hours in the air and days at sea, getting to the Arctic was ridiculously easy. An overnight Finnair flight to Helsinki from JFK in New York, followed by a shuttle to Rovaniemi, which is located in Lapland, the part of Finland famous for its reindeer. The next morning I hopped on a municipal bus that deposited me at the Arctic Circle. I knew this because there was a big sign and a line in the concrete indicating as much. This, Michael Palin had joked while

visiting here to shoot one of his BBC travel documentaries, was
"where twenty-four-hour darkness ends, and twenty-four-hour
merchandising begins." A group of Japanese tourists were already
there, posing and smiling as they took photos and videos of each
other standing in the Arctic, before heading into the many gift
shops in the village. I then got to meet with a very authentic-
looking, fluent-English-speaking, and good-natured Santa Claus,
who told me he admired the discipline of runners but could never
run a marathon in his bulky Santa boots. "Look at them," he said,
pointing to a large square toe sticking out from under his red
robes. "They're not made for distance."

Hours later, I was back at Santa's Village for the 8 P.M. start
of the half marathon, which wound its way along pedestrian paths
through the pine forests of Lapland to the city of Rovaniemi. The
field of two hundred quickly broke up, and I was running alone,
just under seven minutes per mile. At about 15K (9.3 miles), we
came to a fork in the road. There was no sign, no volunteer
pointing the way. I followed the main road, since going straight
would have meant continuing on a narrow path. *Mistake.* I continued for about another mile and hit a dead end. Standing alone
in the middle of the road, I cursed loudly, my one-word epithet
echoing through the woods. Just then a bicyclist came pedaling
furiously down the road. "Hello!" the rider cried, in heavily
accented English. "You go wrong way, please!" She had been out
for a ride when someone told her a runner had gone the wrong
way, and she cycled to my rescue. I followed her back, but my race
was ruined. I ran the last 5K with a scowl on my face, ignoring
the cheering spectators, the children with hands raised for high
fives. After crossing the finish line in Rovaniemi's town square, I
slammed my hat on the ground, bawled out a race official, and

stomped angrily back to my hotel. My time—a 1:37 instead of the 1:31 it should have been. Then I had a vision of Santa looking down at me. He didn't seem quite as jolly as he had this morning; indeed, he looked ready to stomp me with those big boots. A wave of guilt and shame swept over me. Some Christmas spirit. I should be finding the Good Samaritan on the bicycle and thanking her, not sulking in my hotel room over a stupid six-minute differential in a finish time.

I didn't locate her, but I did find something in myself. The anger subsided. Back out to the town square I went, in a very different mood. I lustily cheered the full marathoners struggling in. I bought pints of lager for people gathered to watch the race at an outdoor café and I left generous tips for the barman. I sang along with heavy metal songs blasting from the speakers outside. "Yeah, you . . . shook me all night *lonngggg*!" I bellowed along with AC/DC as the whole town of Rovaniemi came alive at midnight. Back at the hotel I sent an e-mail to my wife and son and told them I missed them. I went to bed, with the sun still shining, a much happier man. The next morning as I stood outside the hotel waiting for the airport shuttle, the race director came running up, apologizing for the course not being properly marked. Before I could interrupt him to say it was I who should apologize for having been angry, he whipped out of his bag a large, impressive-looking trophy. "I wanted to make sure you got this," he said. "You won third place in your age group." This, despite the wrong turn; it was a little miracle on Rovaniemi's equivalent of Thirty-Fourth Street. I was pleased, but as I winged off and left Lapland behind me, I thought again about how far, in every way, I was from Antarctica. Brewpubs, buses, heavy metal, young people crowding the city streets. The Arctic . . . or at least this part of it . . . was closer to Georgetown than to King George Island.

While I had enjoyed my time with Santa and the race, a part of me still felt the unsatisfied call to something epic. I thought of my days on the Southern Ocean, each rise and fall of the *Vavilov* a cosmic nod to my insignificance in a wondrous world, a world that it took me more than half a lifetime to finally discover. Could there ever be anything like that for me again? Or would the remainder of my adventure-running career consist of watching National Geographic specials on my treadmill? On the flight home, I looked out at an awe-inspiring vista of white-capped mountains. It looked like Antarctica! "Greenland," said the passenger next to me. "Beautiful, isn't it?" I nodded in agreement, but my mind was already on the run. I was wondering if somewhere down there they had a marathon.

Acknowledgments

Without those involved in staging the 2005 Antarctica Marathon—principally Thom Gilligan and his staff at Marathon Tours and our expedition leaders from Peregrine Adventures—there would have been no race to run, no book to write. A special thanks to Patrice Malloy, for her cheerful and quick response to our incessant demands for facts, figures, names, and results.

I must also thank my fellow runners, whose company I enjoyed on that trip and whose stories I am honored to tell in these pages. The same goes for the many participants of earlier and more recent editions of the race. They all tell me that running a marathon in Antarctica is something they will never forget, and obviously haven't, at least so far.

My travel to Antarctica and the time needed to research and write this book were supported by a grant from my college, the New York Institute of Technology in Old Westbury. Thanks to Professors Jim Fauvell and Rob Sherwin, Dean Roger Yu, Aca-

demic Affairs vice president Richard Pizer (who has his own
Antarctic connection), and the ISRC Grant committee for their
support of this and all my writing endeavors.

The Scott Polar Research Institute at the University of Cambridge is the world's foremost repository of all knowledge Antarctic. The Institute graciously provided valuable materials, including
several journal articles on the largely forgotten history of exploration in the South Shetland Islands. A special thanks to the Institute's librarian, Heather Lane, and information assistant Shirley
Sawtell.

As part of my research I read many books from the hefty shelf
of Antarctic literature, a number of which are cited in the text.
Absent a formal bibliography, here are a few that made the greatest impression; I heartily recommend them to anyone interested
in this part of the world: Sara Wheeler's marvelous *Terra Incognita*, David Thomson's *Scott, Shackleton, and Amundsen: Ambition
and Tragedy in the Antarctic*, Roff Smith's *Life on the Ice: No One
Goes to Antarctica Alone*, David Crane's *Scott of the Antarctic*, and
Roland Huntford's controversial but classic *The Last Place on Earth*
were all great and instructive reads. Other very fine books and
articles—on Antarctica, the race, and marathon running in
general—were consulted as well, and are cited in the text.

Many Antarctic Web sites provided valuable information, too,
the best and most accessible being www.70south.com.

I wrote a number of articles on the Antarctica Marathon after
my return, some of which provided the basis of stories and anec-
dotes related in the book. I am grateful to all the editors I worked
with (and in many cases continue to work with) at *AARP Bulletin*,
the *Boston Globe Magazine*, *Newsday*, *Runner's World*, and *Smith-*

sonian. They include Carey Winfrey, Jim Toedtman, Susan Crowley, Doug Most, Katie Neitz, Marjorie Robins, and Kari Granville.

Thanks, as always, to my wise agent, Linda Konner, and thanks to Yuval Taylor, my editor at Chicago Review Press. Like the coach you want to scream at during practice and hug afterward, Yuval pushed me to do my best, and I am grateful for that. Also thanks to CRP project editor Devon Freeny, he of the eagle eye and smooth edits. My good friends and fellow scribes Adam Bean, John Capouya, and James O'Brien deserve particular thanks for their special contributions to the book. Also, thanks to Ron Watters at Idaho State, for sharing with us his interesting ideas.

As usual, I thank all my running buddies for listening to these stories as I talked them out on morning runs. Above all, thanks to my family—Donna and Andrew—for their love and support, and for putting up with a husband and dad who disappeared for two weeks in the middle of the school year to run a marathon in Antarctica and then spent much of the subsequent three years immersed in it.

For those interested in participating or learning more about upcoming editions of the Antarctica Marathon, visit www.marathontours.com. For information on the Antarctic Ice Marathon, visit www.icemarathon.com; and to learn about the Last Desert stage race, see www.4deserts.com/ thelastdesert. For those curious about Antarctic adventure minus the marathon part, visit www.peregrineadventures.com.

APPENDIX

Antarctica Marathon 2005 Results
February 26, 2005

FULL MARATHON

Darryn Zawitz	35	M	USA	3:49:19
Michael Dukart	30	M	USA	3:59:38
William Farrell	47	M	USA	4:01:04
John Brust	33	M	USA	4:08:21
Brian Gaines	38	M	USA	4:11:49
James Lawrence	35	M	USA	4:12:25
Janos Kis	40	M	HUN	4:18:25
Michael Brown	45	M	USA	4:20:24
Peter Reed	54	M	GBR	4:21:26
Timothy Rumford	41	M	USA	4:24:45
Harry Noble	58	M	SCO	4:26:03
Jeffrey Smedsrud	46	M	USA	4:31:50
Alyn Park	53	F	USA	4:33:28
Jeffrey Patterson	35	M	USA	4:39:16
Craig Bizjak	43	M	USA	4:39:45
Ivan Field	41	M	GBR	4:40:16
John Hanc	50	M	USA	4:42:00
Kal Bittianda	39	M	USA	4:42:57
Richard Hallworth	49	M	USA	4:45:09
Karen Zacharias	25	F	USA	4:45:39
Annie Hotwagner	42	F	USA	4:45:57

Keith Culver	57	M	USA	4:46:04
Jeffrey Miller	44	M	USA	4:46:30
Patrick Canonica	56	M	USA	4:50:56
Karl Higgins	49	M	USA	4:51:09
Jeremy Trinidad	35	M	USA	4:51:13
Robert Burke	47	M	USA	4:51:41
Ingrid Hall	38	F	GBR	4:57:56
Wendy Lageman	46	F	USA	4:58:36
Vladimir Gladkov	55	M	RUS	5:01:10
Richard Holmes	55	M	USA	5:01:28
Lisa Ramshaw	42	F	CAN	5:01:55
John Wall	49	M	USA	5:02:58
David Weinhold	28	M	USA	5:04:21
Lee Weinhold	56	M	USA	5:04:21
Mark Sinclair	24	M	GBR	5:06:43
Francis Staples	65	M	GBR	5:07:27
Peter Hills	54	M	NZL	5:08:19
James O'Connell	46	M	CAN	5:09:01
Jeffrey Turner	49	M	USA	5:10:58
Jorge Gonzalez	38	M	ESP	5:11:54
Ian Talbot	58	M	GBR	5:12:35
Andrew Witte	35	M	USA	5:14:54
Diane Harty	49	F	USA	5:16:03
Wayne Wright	56	M	USA	5:17:16
John Martens	35	M	USA	5:19:37
Aksel Lovenholm	63	M	NOR	5:19:39
Dennis McGurk	57	M	USA	5:20:39
Mark Ferguson	40	M	USA	5:20:47
Michelle Huddleston	38	F	USA	5:20:50
Morgan Davis	28	M	USA	5:20:56
Richard Griffiths	38	M	GBR	5:21:10
Ellyn Brown	52	F	USA	5:21:27

Richard Ervais	45	M	USA	5:21:53
Adam Oviatt	23	M	USA	5:22:49
Michael Davidson	32	M	GBR	5:26:30
Linda Varoli	34	F	USA	5:26:46
George Andersen	62	M	USA	5:29:00
Jeff Rochford	43	M	USA	5:29:06
Leonard Gibely	51	M	USA	5:29:15
Stephen Camp	42	M	NZL	5:29:53
James Overfelt	41	M	USA	5:30:45
John Walker Jr.	45	M	USA	5:31:01
Mark Burgess	42	M	CAN	5:33:00
William Wrobel	45	M	USA	5:34:39
Timothy Powell	34	M	USA	5:34:52
Arcadi Alibes Riera	45	M	ESP	5:36:24
William Jennings	66	M	USA	5:36:36
Scott Grigsby	45	M	USA	5:38:28
Robert Patton	39	M	GBR	5:39:56
Jay Wissot	60	M	USA	5:40:30
Tamara Grigsby	44	F	USA	5:41:28
Geoffrey Simons	31	M	USA	5:44:10
Nicholas Simonelli	53	M	USA	5:45:04
Michael Fleming	51	M	CAN	5:56:43
Paulus Heule	40	M	USA	5:47:10
Glynis Hadden	45	F	CAN	5:49:43
Elizabeth Spence	48	F	USA	5:53:33
Lisa Lawrence	44	F	USA	5:53:33
William Garrison	41	M	USA	5:54:00
Eric Stover	46	M	USA	5:54:05
Eileen Jessop	40	F	GBR	5:54:19
Karon Van Winkle	44	F	USA	5:55:33
Richard Dziurdzuk	57	M	USA	5:56:40
Clyde Shank	57	M	USA	5:57:14

John Goldrosen	54	M	USA	5:57:39
Mary Hayes	32	F	USA	5:58:09
Michelle Albovias	30	F	USA	5:59:14
Richard D. Hammond	54	M	USA	6:01:03
Tomislav Djurdjevich	34	M	USA	6:03:30
Michael Ripp	38	M	USA	6:04:36
Christopher Brust	27	M	USA	6:05:21
Mitchell Lewis	47	M	USA	6:07:13
Patrick Arsenault	33	M	CAN	6:07:52
Berendinus Klaver	65	M	CAN	6:07:54
Michelle Schall	38	F	USA	6:08:21
Gerald Seddon	60	M	USA	6:08:34
Roger Biggs	56	M	GBR	6:09:07
Radley Geoke	36	M	USA	6:10:53
Donald Lawrence	59	M	USA	6:11:17
Betty Holder	46	F	USA	6:13:22
Cheryl Read	36	F	USA	6:13:53
Ronald Bucy	60	M	USA	6:14:07
Fiona Wright	42	F	USA	6:17:48
Karen Michelsen	40	F	CAN	6:19:17
Kathryn Charles	32	F	GBR	6:19:19
J. Joseph Hale Jr.	55	M	USA	6:20:50
Andrew McBrien	30	M	USA	6:21:27
Reto Cavelti	64	M	SUI	6:21:35
Shannon Bennett	28	F	USA	6:21:49
Rudy Smith	62	M	USA	6:22:00
Julia Fretschl	46	F	USA	6:22:03
Stephen Forte	33	M	USA	6:22:48
Dennis Martin	58	M	USA	6:23:02
Christopher Murdy	47	M	CAN	6:23:46
Marina Jean	32	F	USA	6:24:27
Mortimer Ames	43	M	USA	6:24:28

Yon Ough	60	M	USA	6:25:44
Jeannette McAffer	42	F	CAN	6:26:46
Barbara Wintroub	58	F	USA	6:27:00
Ming Liu	49	M	HKG	6:27:13
Karen Utterback	52	F	USA	6:30:17
Susan Jorth	42	F	USA	6:30:23
Fritz Pieper	39	M	USA	6:31:45
Craig Wanner	53	M	USA	6:31:56
Robert Sweetman	45	M	USA	6:32:02
Edwin Apel Jr.	55	M	USA	6:32:55
Andrea Sarah Ames	36	F	USA	6:34:02
Whit Gregg	57	M	USA	6:35:06
Amy Mills	34	F	USA	6:38:06
Richard Stonebraker	54	M	USA	6:38:37
Brook Kravitz-Ellard	26	F	USA	6:41:50
Sharlene Anderson	56	F	USA	6:42:21
Gary Baron	46	M	CAN	6:43:28
Stephanie Becker	39	F	USA	6:44:28
John Rankin	61	M	CAN	6:45:26
Justin Lawson	23	M	IRL	6:45:28
Michael Weingarten	53	M	USA	6:46:13
Paul Nelson	34	M	USA	6:46:31
Joan Thomas	50	F	USA	6:49:13
Catherine Nelson	30	F	USA	6:49:31
James Ross	18	M	USA	6:51:13
David Ross	55	M	USA	6:51:13
Ty Christian	28	M	USA	6:53:15
Veronica Richards	42	F	USA	6:53:17
Jarrett Roberts	37	M	USA	6:53:20
Karen Nicholson	39	F	USA	6:54:07
Jodi Mueller	32	F	USA	6:54:07
Esther Morris	34	F	USA	6:54:07

Amanda Payne	51	F	GBR	6:54:07
Michael Rucker	32	M	USA	6:54:19
Richard T. Hammond	31	M	USA	6:56:16
Sharon Guttenberger	43	F	USA	6:59:16
Debra Iketani	52	F	USA	7:01:01
Leroy Lightfoot	61	M	USA	7:03:21
Michael Gaar	50	M	USA	7:03:58
Judy Crowson	60	F	USA	7:04:10
Joan Gaar	44	F	USA	7:06:58
Carolyn Krumrey	43	F	USA	7:07:02
Jeffery Thode	40	M	USA	7:07:04
Phillip Webster	47	M	USA	7:08:21
Angelique Webster	40	F	USA	7:11:21
Mieka Gerard	54	F	USA	7:16:57
John Bell	47	M	USA	7:18:09
Lawrence Meyer	57	M	USA	7:25:31
Nels Bentson	60	M	USA	7:26:55
Joel Dunford	48	M	USA	7:34:04
Frans de Vin	56	M	NED	7:36:30
Jason Lawson	25	M	IRL	7:37:01
Colleen Sproul	45	F	USA	7:37:04
Laura Garrett	48	F	USA	7:40:01
Thomas Briggs	71	M	USA	7:47:00
Daniel Powell	45	M	USA	7:53:43
Nita Kay LeMay	52	F	USA	8:00:12
Della Works	60	F	USA	8:00:12
Bobbie Lopresti-Lopez	40	F	USA	8:02:14

HALF MARATHON

Jane Serues	57	F	USA	2:13:08
Segio Cuadra Espinoza	34	M	CHI	2:20:58
Jenny Hadfield	37	F	USA	2:23:39
Patricio Gajardo Aguirre	27	M	CHI	2:34:57
Susan Kirch	50	F	USA	2:52:39
Cesar Cartes Arancibia	30	M	CHI	2:54:19
Jan Nielsen	42	M	DEN	2:59:33
Jorge Guzman Pedraza	32	M	CHI	3:04:18
Darren Bennett	30	M	USA	3:05:07
Mauricio Martinez Perez	39	M	CHI	3:05:34
Christian Espinosa Narvaez	39	M	CHI	3:14:10
Elisha Huricks	39	F	USA	3:18:04
Sayulita Robinson	24	F	USA	3:19:13
Willaim Krumrey	43	M	USA	3:23:05
Richard Koppe	51	M	USA	3:25:32
Peggy Slendorn	42	F	USA	3:25:32
Alex Sinadino	57	M	USA	3:25:52
Rosemary Hager-Heule	40	F	USA	3:26:32
Harvey Organek	55	M	USA	3:29:02
Monica Martin	39	F	USA	3:33:09
Charles Monahan	65	M	USA	3:43:00
Linda Rigney	34	F	USA	3:43:57
Shareen Worth	54	F	USA	3:53:36
Paul Zacharias	56	M	USA	4:04:10
Virginia Turner	52	F	USA	4:08:39
Rohitkumar Vasa	57	M	USA	4:11:03
Jay Foonberg	69	M	USA	4:12:42
Monica Ann Bell	32	F	USA	4:12:55
Carol Kettlewell	53	F	USA	4:52:27

Susan Sinclair	52	F	USA	4:52:52
Laura Johnson	77	F	CAN	4:57:31
Barney Thomas	53	M	USA	5:16:21
Kathleen Wanner	50	F	USA	5:17:28
Suzanne Bressler	36	F	USA	5:40:10
David Foonberg	37	M	USA	5:43:22
William Tan	47	M	SIN	5:50:41

Index